Elisha Albright Hoffman, John Harrison Tenney

Spiritual Songs for Gospel Meetings and the Sunday School

Elisha Albright Hoffman, John Harrison Tenney

Spiritual Songs for Gospel Meetings and the Sunday School

ISBN/EAN: 9783337334840

Printed in Europe, USA, Canada, Australia, Japan

Cover: Foto ©Thomas Meinert / pixelio.de

More available books at **www.hansebooks.com**

SPIRITUAL SONGS

FOR

GOSPEL MEETINGS

AND THE

SUNDAY SCHOOL,

BY

REV. ELISHA A. HOFFMAN,

AND J. H. TENNEY.

PUBLISHED BY

BARKER & SMELLIE,

35 Superior and 45 Union Streets,

CLEVELAND, O.

TO JESUS,

OUR PRECIOUS REDEEMER, who is the theme of our song, and to the FRIENDS OF THE MASTER, who love his appearing, and delight to sing his praise, these

"Spiritual Songs"

Are consecrated, in the hope that the Saviour may be glorified in them, that his people may be comforted, blessed, quickened and strengthened, and that some erring souls may be won to the Cross thereby.

THE BOOK IS ADAPTED FOR

Gospel Meetings,	*Sunday Schools,*	*Prayer Meetings,*
Conventions,	*Camp Meetings,*	*Institutes,*
Y. M. C. A. Meetings,	*Assemblies,*	
Mission Churches, &c.,		

And wherever song is used as an element of worship. In humble conse-cration, we lay the book at the feet of the blessed Master.

"**W**ITH grateful hearts, O Lord, we bring
These psalms, and hymns, and songs to thee;
Content to serve in anything,
So we may but thy servants be.

Accept and bless the songs we sing,
And tune our souls to loftier strains,
So we may join the notes that ring
Triumphant o'er the heavenly plains."—H. B. H.

" Unto him who loved us, and washed us from our sins in his own blood, and hath made us kings and priests unto God and his Father; to him be glory and dominion for ever and ever, Amen."

ELISHA A. HOFFMAN,
J. H. TENNEY.

SELECTIONS FOR EXAMINATION.

NEW SONGS—7, 9, 15, 19, 22, 29, 31, 32, 45, 52, 58, 70, 71, 77, 80.

NEW SONGS BY P. P. BLISS—3, 4, 17, 33, 66, 69.

SONGS ALREADY POPULAR—5, 6, 8, 11, 14, 25, 34, 38, 43, 49, 50, 54, 59, 61, 64, 67, 68, 70, 78, 81.

SPIRITUAL SONGS.

The Shadow Of The Cross.

Dr. H. Bonar.   P. P. Bliss, by per.

1. Op - press'd with noon - day's scorch - ing heat, To
2. Be - neath that cross clear wa - ters burst, A

yon - der cross I flee; Be - neath its shel - ter
foun - tain spark - ling free; And there I quench my

take my seat; No shade like this for me!
des - ert thirst; No spring like this for me!

Fine.

Refrain.   *D.S.*

No shade like this for me, ... No shade like this for me! ...
No spring like this for me, ... No spring like this for me! ...

No shade like this for me, ... like this for me.
No spring like this for me, ... like this for me.

3. A stranger here, I pitch my tent
   Beneath this spreading tree:
   Here shall my pilgrim life be spent;
   No home like this for me!

4. For burden'd ones a resting place
   Beside that cross I see;
   I here cast off my weariness;
   No rest like this for me!

Abundantly Able To Save.

E. A II   P. P. Bliss.

1. Who-ev-er re - ceiv - eth the Cru-ci-fied One,   Who-ev-er be-
2. Who-ev-er re - ceiv - eth the message of God.   And trusts in the
3. Who-ev-er re - pents   and forsakes every sin,   And opens his

liev - eth on God's on-ly Son.   A free and a   per - fect
pow'r   of the soul-cleansing blood. A full and e - ter - nal
heart   for the Lord to come in,   A present and per - fect

salvation shall have,   For he is a - bun - dant-ly a - ble to save.
redemption shall have, For he is both a   -   ble and willing to save.
salvation shall have,   For Jesus is read - y this moment to save.

Chorus.

My brother! the Mas - - ter is call-ing for thee;   His grace and his
Brother, the Master is come and is calling for thee,

mer - - cy are wondrously free;   His blood as a ran - - som
Brother, his grace and his mercy are wondrously free,   Brother, his blood as

for sinners he gave,   And he is a - bun - dantly a - ble to save.
a ransom for sinners he gave,   And he is abundantly able to save.

Toiling Up The Way.

Moderato.   Arr. by JNO. R. SWENEY, by per.

1. We are toiling up the way, Narrow way, narrow way; We have
   T'ward the distant shining land, Golden land, golden land, Where the
2. Tho' the journey may be long, Hard and long, hard and long, We will
   We shall en-ter by the cross, Blessed cross, blessed cross, Gain-ing

Chorus.

journey'd many a day T'ward the kingdom; }
heav'nly harpers stand In the king-dom. } Still we sing, Christ, our King,
cheer it with a song Of the king-dom; }
gold that hath no dross, In the king-dom. }

Walks with us the wea-ry way,   And the shining angels wait, an-gels

wait, an-gels wait, To un-bar the golden gate Of the king - dom.

The Lord Is My Light.

JAMES NICHOLSON.　　　　From "Crystal Songs," by per　　　　J. W. BISCHOFF.

1. The Lord is my light, then why should I fear? By day and by night His
2. The Lord is my light, though clouds may arise; Faith stronger than sight looks
3. The Lord is my light, the Lord is my strength: I know in His might I'll
4. The Lord is my light, my all and in all; There is in His sight no

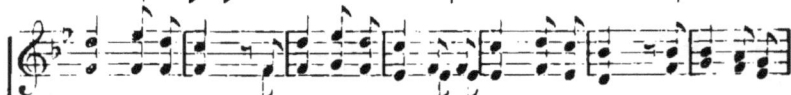

pres-ence is near; He is my salvation from sorrow and sin; This blessed per-
up to the skies; When Je-sus for-ev-er in glo-ry doth reign, Then how can I
con-quer at length; My weakness in mercy He covers with power, And walking by
darkness at all; He is my Redeemer, my Saviour and King; With saints and with

Chorus.

sua - sion the Spir - it brings in.　　The Lord is my light, my
ev - er in dark - ness remain?
faith He saves me each hour.
an - gels His prais-es I sing.

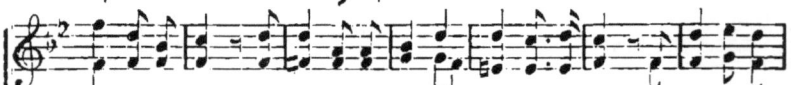

joy and my song; By day and by night He leads me along, The Lord is my

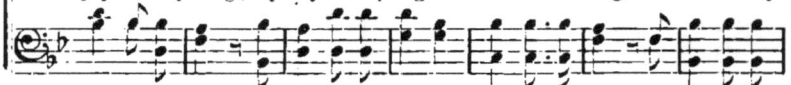

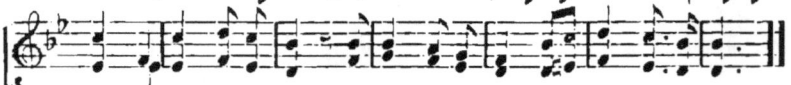

light, my joy and my song: By day and by night He leads me along.

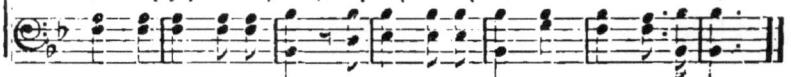

I Will Trust My Redeemer.

Rev. H. B. Hartzler.   W. A. Galpin.

1. I will live for my Re-deem-er— Once He lived on earth for
2. I will walk with my Re-deem-er, With Him bear and suf-fer
3. I will work for my Re-deem-er— Once He toiled on earth for

me; And He lives for me in glo - ry, Pleased my
pain, That I may re - ceive the prom - ise: With Him
me; And for Him in faith-ful la - bor, Day by

faith - ful toil to see;
on His throne to reign.
day I long to be.

Chorus.

I will trust my dear Re-

deem - er; I will love Him more and more; I will

fol - low till I meet Him On yon fair, e - ter-nal shore.

Precious Name.

Rev. I. BALTZELL, by per

1. Precious is the name of Je - sus, Who can half its worth unfold, For be-
2. Precious as the Me-di - a - tor, By the Fath-er raised on high, Precious,
3. Precious when to Calvary groan-ing, He sustained the cursed tree ; Precious,
4. Precious when in death vic-tor - ious, He the hosts of hell o'erthrows: In His
.5. Precious Lord, beyond ex-press-ing Are thy beauties all di-vine ; Glo-ry,

yond an - gel - ic prais - es, Sweetly sung to harps of gold.
when he took our na - ture, Laid his aw - ful glo-ry by.
when His death a - ton - ing, Made an end of sin for me.
re - sur - rec-tion glo - rious Vic - tor crowned o'er all his foes.
hon - or, power, and bless - ing, Be henceforth, for-ev - er thine.

Chorus.

Precious name, O how sweet, Precious name, O how
Precious name, O how sweet. Precious name.

Rit. p *Repeat pp*

sweet, Precious name, O how sweet, O how sweet !
O how sweet, Precious name, O how sweet.

Rev. Elisha A. Hoffman.

1st time.

1. Would you know why I love Je - sus? Why he is so dear to me?
'Tis because my bless-ed Je - sus . . . .

2d time.

From my sins has ransomed me.

Chorus.

This is why I love my
This is why I love my Je-sus, This is

Je - - sus, This is why I love him so, He a-
why I love him so, This is why I love my Je-sus, This is why I love him so, He has

toned for my transgres - sions, He has washed me white as snow, white as snow.
pardoned my transgressions, He has pardoned my transgressions, He has washed me, He has made
[me white as snow.

2. Would you know why I love Jesus?
   Why he is so dear to me?
   'Tis because the blood of Jesus
   Fully saves and cleanses me.

3. Would you know why I love Jesus?
   Why he is so dear to me?
   'Tis because, amid temptation,
   He supports and strengthens me.

4. Would you know why I love Jesus?
   Why he is so dear to me?
   'Tis because in every conflict
   Jesus gives me victory.

5. Would you know why I love Jesus?
   Why he is so dear to me?
   'Tis because, my friend and Savior
   He will ever, ever be.

Lead Me To Jesus.

"And Jesus stood and commanded him to be brought unto him."—Luke 18: 40.

E. D. M.   T. C. O'KANE.

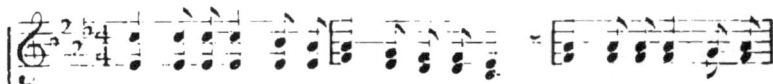

1 Lead me to Je - sus, my soul is so wea-ry.   Wea - ry of bear-ing the
2. Mountains impassable, sins rise around me.   Hiding the light of the
3. Lead me to Je - sus, my soul now returning,   Seeks in his bosom its

yoke of sin; Dark clouds above me, my pathway is dreary, Joy never dwells my sad
Father's face : Sitting in darkness, sin fetters have bound me, Vainly I struggle with
resting-place : Lead me to Jesus, my heart now is burning, Longing for mercy, and

Chorus.

heart within. Lead me to Jesus, lead me to-day ; Lead me to Jesus, lead me I pray:
out his grace.
love, and grace.

Tenderly, carefully, Lovingly, prayerfully. Lead me to Je - sus.

From "Heavenly Carols," by per.

Why Don't You Come To Jesus?

C. R. Dunham, by per.

1. Je - sus now is my sal-va - tion, He has saved me from all sin;
Thro' his blood I have re-demp - tion, ...
2. By his royal pro-cla-ma - tion, Sin's do-min-ion now is o'er,
And in conscious full sal-va - tion . . . .
3. Oh, the love of my Re-deem - er! Oh, the wonders of his grace!
I will praise his name forever, ...

And I rest complete in him.
I may sing forever-more.
And rejoice before his face.

Semi-Chorus.

O the joy of full sal-va - tion!
Spread the news to every na - tion:

How it thrills my inmost soul!

Je - sus blood has made me whole.

Full Chorus. p   m   f

Why don't you come to Je-sus? why don't you come to Je-sus? why

don't you come to Je-sus and be saved? . . saved?

The Savior's Call.

Words and Music by CHAS. H. GABRIEL.

1. At the door I'm knocking, knocking, Will you rise and let me in?
2. At the door I'm knocking, knocking, But the door is hard to move;
3. At the door I'm knocking, knocking, But I'm wait-ing all in vain;
4. At the door I'm knocking, knocking, Must I, must I now de-part?

I am waiting, on-ly waiting To forgive your every sin.
For the rus-ty hinges give not, While I wait in hope and love.
Closely is the i-vy clinging; Will the door unbarred remain?
For so much, so much I love you, And I want your weary heart.

Chorus

voice of Je-sus call-ing, While his heart in pit-y bleeds; Will you

o-pen wide the door way, While so ten-der-ly he pleads?

Hiding In The Rock.

Rev. H. B. Hartzler.   Chas. H. Gabriel.

1. In the Rock of A-ges hid - ing, I have found a sure re-
2. In the Rock of A-ges rest - ing, I en-joy a sweet re-
3. In the Rock of A-ges trust - ing, I am kept in per-fect

treat; In the Refuge now a-bid - ing, I have found a joy complete.
pose, Where the grace of God for-ev - er Like a mighty riv-er flows.
peace; In the hope of glo-ry wait - ing, Till the toil of life shall cease.

Chorus.

While the storm a-round me rag - es, And the an-gry bil-lows roar, I am hid-ing in the Rock of A - ges, I am safe for-ev - er-more.

Evergreen Plain.

Rev. I. BALTZELL, by per.

1. Shall we meet beyond the river, In that clime where angels dwell? Shall we
2. Shall we meet where flow'rs are blooming, Ever fadeless, ever fair, Where the
3. Shall we meet our loved companions, On that brighter, fairer shore? When this
4. Yes! we'll meet beyond the river, Where our joys shall never die, We shall

meet where friendship never,   Sad-dest tales of sor - row   tell?
light of day il - lum-ines,   Lives of those who en-ter   there?
life's great work is ended,   Shall we meet to part no   more?
meet our lov'd and lost ones,   In that hap - py by and   by.

Chorus.

Shall we meet,.......... shall we meet,...... Shall we meet on the evergreen
Shall we meet,   shall we meet,

Rit.

plain? Shall we meet and know each other ever, Shall we never part again?

E. A. H.   E. A. H.

1. Have you been to Jesus for the cleans-ing pow'er? Are you
2. Are you walk-ing dai-ly by the Sav-ior's side? Are you
3. When the Bridegroom cometh, will your robes be white, Pure and
4. Lay a-side the garments that are stained with sin, And be

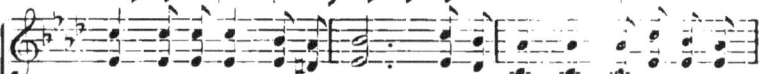

washed in the blood of the Lamb? Are you ful-ly trusting in his
washed in the blood of the Lamb? Do you rest each moment in the
white in the blood of the Lamb? Will your soul be read-y for the
washed in the blood of the Lamb? There's a foun-tain flowing for the

Chorus.

grace this hour? Are you washed in the blood of the Lamb?   Are you
Cru-ci-fied? Are you washed in the blood of the Lamb?
man-sions bright, And be washed in the blood of the Lamb?
soul un-clean, O be washed in the blood of the Lamb!

washed   in the blood, In the soul-cleansing blood of the Lamb? Are your

Are you washed   in the blood   of the Lamb?

gar-ments spotless? Are they white as snow? Are you washed in the blood of the Lamb?

The Wanderer's Prayer.

Rev. E. W. Lawton.   (May be sung as a Solo.)   J. H. Tenney, by per.

1. O Lord! I come once more to thee, To seek thy smile of peace; From
2. When I remember all my sin Against thy law and grace, And
3. Let not the foe my heart deceive, Forgive-ness is in store; O

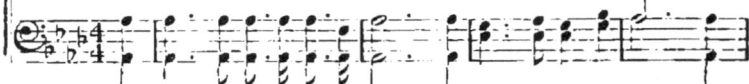

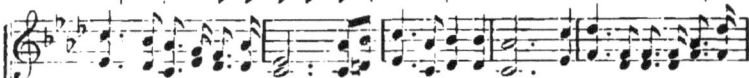

all the pow'rs of sin I flee, From all its ways I'd cease. A thousand earnest vows I've
see how false my heart has been, I fear to seek thy face; My trembling soul sinks in de-
let me now look up, believe, Believe, and sin no more! Thy word demands of feeble

made, And brok-en every one, But let me plead the precious blood Of
spair Beneath the heavy load; All faith is taken from my prayer; I
dust Forgiveness full and free, And, surely, thou who art so just Will

Chorus.

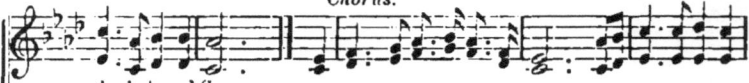

thy beloved Son.
stand condemned of God.   O Sav-ior! help me to believe, Believe, and sin no
fully pardon me.

more; Nor e'er, again, thy Spirit grieve, But love thee ev-er-more.

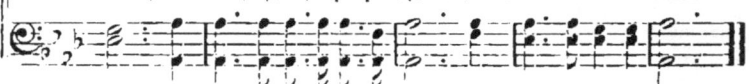

Rev. H. B. Hartzler.

P. P. Bliss.

1. Precious is the blood of the Lamb that was slain ; Precious is the heart that was
2. Precious is the Love that is might-ty to save ; Precious is the Light that il-
3. Precious are the pleadings of Je · sus for me ; Precious are the lips that have

broken in twain ; Precious are the hands that were nailed to the tree ; Precious are the
lumines the grave ; Precious is the Truth that is changless and sure ; Precious is the
spoken me free ; Precious are the tears that he wept in the strife ; Precious is the

Chorus.

feet that were wounded for me.
Life that is endless and pure.   Glo-ry to the Lamb! Oh, glory to the Lamb!
death that has purchased my life.

For the precious blood he   shed   on the tree; Glo-ry   to the Lamb! Oh,
For the precious, precious blood he shed upon the tree,

glo - ry   to the Lamb!   For the precious life   he   gave   un - to me.

2

For What Are You Waiting?

GRACE MELBOURNE.

W. IRVING HARTSHORN.

1. For what are you waiting, my brother, As you journey thro' life's vale of
2. For what are you waiting, my brother? O why are you waiting in
3. The Father keeps watch o'er his children, And knows who has garnered the

tears? You are wast-ing the glo-ri-ous sun-shine, And
vain? For oth-ers are work-ing in pa-tience, And
grain; O what will you do when he tells you Your

Chorus.

los-ing the harv-est of years.
reap-ing and bind-ing the grain. O why stand you i-dle and
hope of yon heav-en is vain.

wait-ing to-day? Your hands have a work to do; The Mas-ter will

come! If your sheaves are not ready, What hope of yon heaven have you, have you?

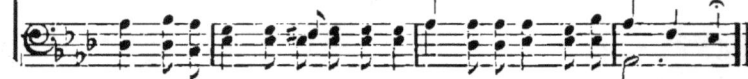

E. A. H.   E. A. H.

1. Though our burdens may be heavy, yet they all seem light, When we
2. Let us all be true to Je-sus, and in meek-ness bear All our

think of what awaits us in the Par-a-dise so bright; Come re-
heav-y, heav-y Cross-es till the glo-ry we may share, 'Till we

proach, or scorn, or sorrow we will faithful be, Till we wear the Crown of life e-
gain the Crown unfading and the robe of white, O-ver in the pal-a-ces of

Chorus.

ter-nal-ly.   Oh! the Cros...... We'll meekly bear,......... And then go
gold-en light.   The blessed Cross,   We'll meekly bear,

1st time.   **2d time.**

home......... a shining Crown to wear, }
And then go home   a Crown to wear, }   A shining Crown to wear.

The Prodigal Coming Home.

H F H   *"And he arose and came to his father."—Luke 15: 20.*   E. S. LORENZ.

1. In the wilds of sin a weary soul astray From the home of love had
2. But he heard a voice in tender mercy say, "Sinner, come, why longer
3. Coming home all faint and hungry, and athirst, To the feast of love and
4. Coming home to seek a blessed mercy seat, With a load of guilt and

gone; Like a poor, lost lamb, he wandered far away, In his grief and woe a-
stay?" And he comes, he comes, along the homeward way, Coming home no more to
peace; Coming home by all the woe of sin accurst, To receive a quick re-
shame, And a contrite heart to lay at Jesus' feet, In the faith of his dear

Chorus.

lone.
stray.   Yes, the prod-i-gal's coming home, Coming home, no more to roam; He is
lease.
name.

weary of wand'ring far away from home; He is seeking his Father's face, he is

longing for his grace, Yes, the prodigal's coming home, coming home.
    coming home.

From "Heavenly Carols," b per.

Mrs. Mary F. Marsh.   Matt. 8: 3.   Rev. W. K. Wland.

1. Touch and cleanse me, blessed Savior, I am wea - ry of my sin,   I am
2. Touch and cleanse me, blessed Savior, Humbly now my guilt I own, Oh be-

longing for thy fa-vor, Longing to be pure within; Touch and cleanse me, blessed
stow thy pard'ning favor! Thou canst save me, thou alone; Thou dost cleanse me, blessed

Savior, I am poor, and weak, and blind, Grant me now thy loving favor. Let me
Savior, Light is streaming from above, Now I feel thy pard'ning favor, Oh, my

Refrain.

now sal-va-tion find! Touch and cleanse me, touch and cleanse me, Listen to my fee-ble
soul is full of love. Thou dost cleanse me, thou dost cleanse me, Thou hast heard my feeble

cry; Touch and cleanse me, touch and cleanse me, Jesus save me or I die.
cry; Thou dost cleanse me, thou dost cleanse me, Glory be to God on high!

That Open Door.

Words from "CENTRAL PRESBYTERIAN." J. H. T.

1. I have longed for the bliss of pardon, And sighed to be cleansed from
2. I will trust, though I walk in darkness, And pray till the light I
3. I have longed for the bliss of pardon, And sighed to be free from

sin; And I know if I come be-liev-ing, My Sav-ior will let me
see, For the blood that has cleansed the vilest, Will sure-ly a-vail for
sin: And I knock at the door believing, That Je - sus will let me

in: For the door of his love is o-pen, He wait-eth for those who
me; I have on - ly the plea to of- fer, That Je - sus for me has
in; Oh, the faith in my soul grows stronger, I tremble with fear no

seek, But I tremble with fear and doubting, Oh, why is my faith so weak?
died, And with only my heart to give Him, I haste to His blessed side.
more, 'Tis my Savior that bids me welcome,—I'll en-ter that open door.

Chorus.

o - pen door, I'll en - ter that o - pen

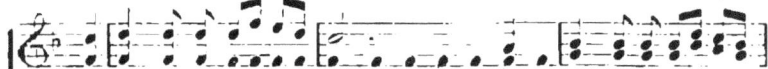

I'll en-ter that open door, I'll enter that open door, I'll en - ter that o-pen

o - pen door, I'll

I'll en-ter that open door, I'll en-ter that o-pen door,

door, 'Tis Je-sus invites, I'll en-ter in, I'll enter that o-pen door.
enter that open door,

Waiting At The Cross.

ELLA CHEEK.   J. H. ANDERSON.

1. Je - sus, I am waiting now, Weary, worn, and weak ; } Peace and rest I
   At the Cross I'm bending low, ...
2. Long I've wandered far from thee, In the paths of sin ; } Je-sus, take me
   Let my sorrow plead for me, ...
3. Chase my heart's unrest away, Bid its troubling cease ; } Give me thy sweet
   Let me feel thy love to-day, ...

D. C. *Speak the blessed words to me,* . . . . . . "*Come, I'll give thee*

Fine.   *Chorus.*   D. C.

seek.
in.
peace.   Je-sus, I am wait-ing now, Longing to be blest,

rest."

From "Joy Bells," by per.

Talking With Jesus.

St. Luke 24: 32.

Adagio Espressivo.

ASA HULL.

1. A little talk with Jesus, How it smooths the rugged road; How it
2. I know the way is drea-ry, To that bright and happy clime; But a
3. I'll tell him I am wea-ry, And I fain would be at rest; That I'm
4. I'll wait a lit - tle longer,—Till his own appointed time; And will

seems to help me onward, When I faint beneath my load. When my heart is crushed with
little talk with Je-sus Will refresh me an-y time. And as yet the more I
dai-ly, hourly long-ing For a home upon his breast. Once he gave his life a
glory in the knowledge Of a prospect so sublime. Then, when in my Fath-er's

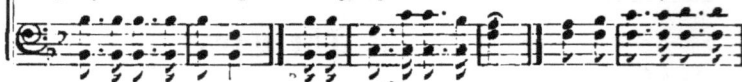

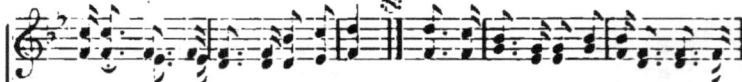

sorrow, And my eyes with tears are dim, There is naught can yield me comfort Like a
know him, And his mercy I ex-plore, Only prompts my heart to longing For a
ransom And would have me all his own. Can he now forget his promise, And re-
dwelling, Where the many "mansions" are, I will sweetly talk with Jesus, And for-

D. S. *There is naught can yield me comfort, Like a*

Fine. *Chorus.* *D. S.*

little talk with him. A little talk with Jesus, How it smooths the rugged road;
little talk the more.
ject his purchased one.
ever dwell up there.—

little talk with God.

From "Garlands of Praise," by per.

God Is Coming.

MRS. SUE M. O. HOFFMAN.

1. God is coming! God is coming! shout aloud the glad re-frain;
2. God is coming! God is coming! roll the notes of joy on high;
3. God is coming! God is coming! and the hosts of sin are strong;
4. God is coming! God is coming! O lift up your hearts and pray!

Fine.

Send the cry from town and cit - y to the vil - lage, ham-let, plain;
Ev - ery blood-bought son of Je-sus, ral - ly to your lead-er's cry!
We will meet them bravely, bold-ly, and the fight will not be long.
In the fight 'twixt light and darkness he will need strong arms to-day.

D.S. Every man be up on du - ty, For Je-hov-ah comes this way.

God is com-ing! hear the an - gels shout the tidings from above;
God is com-ing! God is com-ing! rub your rus-ty ar-mor bright,
God is com-ing! and be-fore him powers of darkness must give way;
God is com-ing! fal - ter nev - er—when the conflict here is done

He will de - luge our whole country with his ti-dal wave of love.
Gird your sword and shield about you, and be read-y for the fight.
God is com-ing! by his strong arm we shall gain the vic-tor-y.
You shall wear a crown of glo-ry in the kingdom of his Son.

Chorus. *D.S.*

God is com-ing! pass the watchword all a-long the line to-day!

If Thou Leadest Me.

"In thy presence is fulness of joy."—Psalms 16: 11.

MRS. E. C. ELLSWORTH.   J. H. T.

1 A-ny-where, dear Je-sus, lead my willing feet. On-ly let me clasp thy hand,
2 A-ny-where, dear Je-sus, on-ly on me smile, Strengthen, guard and comfort me,
3 A-ny-where, dear Je-sus, on - ly this I pray : Keep me in the narrow path,
4 A-ny-where, dear Je-sus, if at last I come, Where I'll see thee face to face

feel thy presence sweet; Thorns may pierce and snares beset, I will follow thee,
let not sin beguile : Dark and toilsome be my way, I will nev-er fear,
nev - er let me stray: Sin may plead with si-ren voice, I will answer nay;
in my heav'nly home ; There are many mansions bright, there remains a rest,

Chorus.

A-ny-where, dear Je-sus, if thou leadest me.
A-ny-where, dear Je-sus, if thy presence cheer.   A-ny-where, dear Je-sus,
Kept by thee, dear Je-sus, I will hold my way.
There with thee, dear Je-sus, I'll be truly blest.

A-ny-where with thee, A-ny-where dear Jesus, If thou lead - est me.

Is My Name Written There?

M. A. K.   FRANK M. DAVIS, by per.

1. Lord, I care not for riches, Neither silver nor gold; I would make sure of
2. Lord, my sins they are many, Like the sands of the sea, But thy blood, Oh, my
3. Oh! that beautiful cit - y, With its mansions of light, With its glo-ri-fied

heaven, I would en - ter the fold'; In the book of thy kingdom, With its
Sav-ior! Is suf - fi-cient for me; For thy promise is written, In bright
be-ings, In pure garments of white; Where no evil thing cometh, To de-

pa-ges so fair, Tell me, Je-sus, my Savior, Is my name written there?
letters that glow, "Though your sins be as scarlet, I will make them like snow."
spoil what is fair; Where the angels are watching,—Is my name written there?

Chorus.

Is my name writ - ten there, On the page white and fair?

In the book of thy king-dom, Is my name writ-ten there?

Work Before Reward.

REV. E. W. LAWHON.   J. H. T.

1. I will not murmur, nor sigh for rest, With earth's broad field in view, The harvest, truly, is
2. The seed was scattered in faith and tears, By toilers true and brave; And now the harvest is
3. Although the tardy and burdened years, Delay my flight above, Each day of labor brings

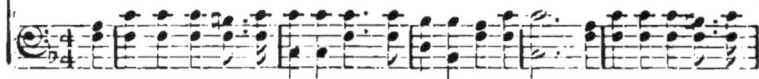

very great, The reapers very few; There is no mansion above for me Until
ripe, while they Are sleeping in the grave; In storms of winter, and summer's heat, They
swift reward Of God's sustaining love; And how much sweeter will be my rest, When

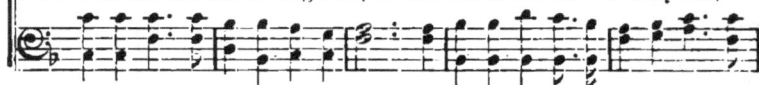

my work is done, The work of patience in this great field, Spread out beneath the sun.
labored in the field; O let us enter with willing hands, And save the golden yield!
I have gained the goal! And how much brighter will be my crown, If I have saved a soul.

Chorus.

Then let us labor on, cheerfully waiting, Trusting the Father's tender love;

Knowing that all the labor in the harvest Brightens the hope of rest above.

Hallelujah! He Redeemed Me.

E. A. H.

E. A. H.

1. The Lord is all in all to me, O help me tell the sto - ry!
For by his blood he ransomed me, And I will give him glo - ry.
2. I am re-deemed, O wondrous grace! The Lord is my sal-va - tion;
Come, join with me his name to praise In songs of ac-cla - ma - tion.
3. My ma - ny stains are washed a-way, My sins are all for-giv - en;
I walk with Christ the narrow way, And find in him my heav - en.

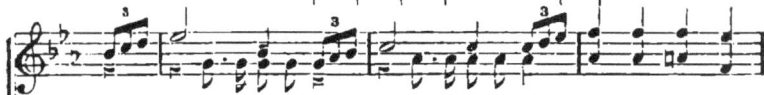

Hal - le - lu - jah! he re - deemed me, O give him all the
Hal-le-lu-jah! He redeemed me,

glo - ry! He shed his blood on Cal - va - ry, Hal-le-

D.S. shed his blood on Cal - va - ry, Hal-le-
Fine.

lu - jah! he re - deemed me. Re-deemed, Re-deemed, Re-

lu - jah! he re - deemed me.

D.S.

deemed, Redeemed, Re-deemed, Redeemed, Re-deemed! He

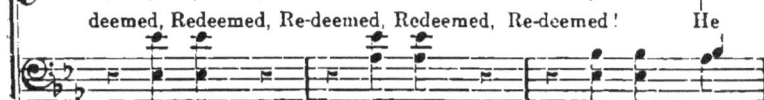

My Precious Bible.

"Thy word is a lamp unto my feet and a light unto my path."— Psalm 119 : 105.

H. B. H.   E. S. LORENZ.

1. Like a Star of the morning in its beau - ty, Like a Sun is the
2. 'Tis a light in the wilderness of sor - row, And a Lamp on the
3. 'Tis the Voice of a Friend forever near me, In the toil and the
4. It shall stand in its beauty and its glo - ry, When the earth and the

Bible to my soul, Shining clear on the way of love and du - ty, As I
weary pilgrim way, And it guides to the bright, e-ter-nal morrow, Shining
battle here be-low; In the gloom of the val-ley it will cheer me, Till the
heavens pass a-way; Ev-er tell-ing the blessed, wondrous sto-ry Of the

D. S. cling to the dear, old, Holy Bi - ble, As I

Fine.   *Chorus.*

hasten on my journey to the goal.
more and more unto the perfect day.   Ho - ly Bi - ble! my precious
glory of His kingdom I shall know.
loving Lamb, the only Living Way.   Ho-ly Bi-ble! Holy Bible! precious

hasten to the Cit-y of the King.

D.S.

Bi - ble! Gift of God, and Lamp of Life, my beautiful Bi - ble! I will
Bible! book divine!   Bible! thou art mine!

From "Heavenly Carols," by per.

CHAS. L. BUTLER.   JNO. R. SWENEY.

1. I was once far a-way from the Sav - ior, And as vile as a
2. But there in that lone - ly hour A voice sweetly
3. Ful-ly then trusted I in Je - sus, And oh, what a

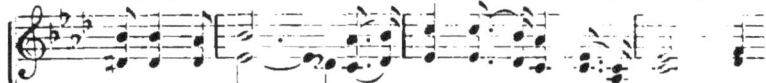

sin-ner could be; I wondered if Christ the Re-deem - er,
whispered to me, Saying, "Christ, the Redeemer, hath pow - er
joy came to me; My heart was filled with prais - es

Would save a poor sinner like me. I wan - dered on in the
To save a poor sinner like thee." I listened, and lo! 'twas the
For he saved a poor sinner like me. No long-er in darkness I'm

dark - ness, Not a ray of light could I see: And the
Sav - ior That was speak-ing so kind to me: I
walk - ing, For the light is shin - ing on me, And

tho't fill'd my heart with sad - ness, There's no hope for a sinner like me.
cried, "I'm the chief of sin - ners, Thou canst save a poor sinner like me."
now un - to others I'm tell - ing How he saved a poor sinner like me.

From "Dew of Hermon," by per.

Coming To Jesus.

Chas. H. Gabriel.
Moderato.

J. H. Tenney.

1. This world, blessed Sav - ior, is nothing but dross, And long we have
2. We long have been try - ing the pleasures of sin; Our hearts in their
3. Tho' wea-ry and foot - sore, we're journeying on, Assured that the

lived without owning thy cross; Now feeling the need of thy sheltering
hard-ness would not let thee in; But now we have found that earth's beauties de-
time of our rest will soon dawn; Then over the riv - er of death we will

arm, We come unto thee to be shielded from harm.
cay, And leave us in sor - row at each fleet-ing day.
go, And leave all our sor - rows and troubles be - low.

Chorus. Faster.
We're coming to thee, we're coming to thee,

Coming to thee, coming to thee, Dear Savior, re-

Coming to thee, com-

ceive us, we're coming to thee, Coming to thee, Oh, receive
we're coming to thee,

Coming To Jesus.—CONCLUDED.

ing to thee, Yes, we're com-ing to thee.

us, we're coming to thee, Yes, we're coming, we're coming, we're coming to thee.

Come To The Cross.

MRS. E. C. ELLSWORTH.   P. P. BLISS.

1. O come to the cross, near the spear-wounded side Where many have wash'd in the
2. O come and be robed in a garment of white, And walk with the Lord as a
3. O come to the feast by the Father prepared, Where thousands of souls in his

sin-cleansing tide! O plunge 'neath the waves, and the bright crimson flow Shall cleanse every
child of the light, Reflecting the glory that shines from his face, And doing his
bounty have shared; O come to the feast, it is costly yet free; There's room, and a

D. S. save thee, He'll

Fine.   Chorus.   D. S.

stain, make thee whiter than the snow!
will in the strength of his grace. O come, then, to Christ! O come, come to-day! He'll
robe, and a welcome for thee.

wash all thy stains of sin away.

Knocking At The Door.

Lizzie Underwood.   James McGranahan, by per.

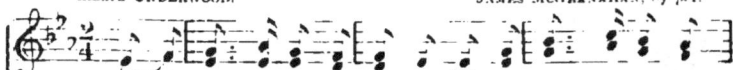

1. Be - hold a stranger stand-ing, Just out - side a close-barr'd
2. I heard His soft voice call-ing, Ev - er call - ing at the
3. Christ is knocking, gent-ly knocking, Ev - er knock-ing at my
4. So we'll ev - er sup to-geth - er, This bless - ed Friend and

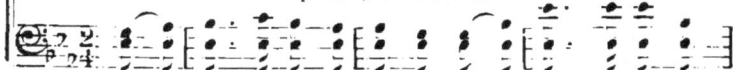

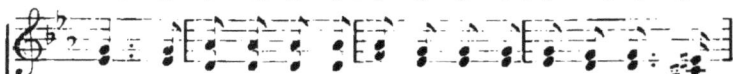

door; He's wea-ry with His wait-ing, But He will not give it
door; I'm knocking, sin - ner, knocking, As I've oft - en knocked be-
heart; I'll glad - ly bid Him en - ter, I will ask Him not de-
I: And if I ev - er hun - ger, He can hear my faint - est

o'er; He knocks, and as He's knocking He lifts His heavenly
fore; Just ope the door a mo-ment, Long e-nough to let me
part; Welcome! welcome! blessed Stranger, Come in and sup with
cry; And when my war-fare's o - ver, I'll share His heav'n-ly

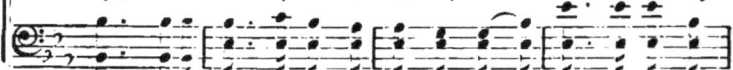

voice, "Ope the door and let me enter; I will make your hearts rejoice."
in, And I'll dwell with you for-ev-er, And will cleanse you from all sin.
me— Ful-fill Thy gracious promise, Lord, And let me sup with Thee.
bliss; Oh, who could ever bar the door 'Gainst such a friend as this?

Chorus.

Knocking, ev - er knock - ing, knocking, ev - er knock - ing,

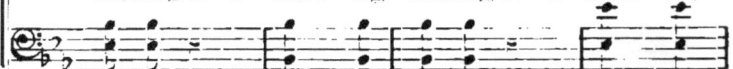

Knocking At The Door.—Concluded.

Knocking At The Door.—Concluded.

Christ is ev-er gen-tly knocking, knocking at the door:

He will leave me nev-er, Dwell with me for-ev-er;

Repeat after last verse pp.

Glad-ly will I bid Him en-ter, And de-part no more.

Send Me Thy Blessing.

JOHN SCOTFORD.

1. There's not upon earth such a hallowed re-treat As where, with a
   We lay all our cares and complaints at the feet Of Jesus, our
2. While conscious of weakness, of want and of sin, And wholly un-
   On Je-sus, the Sav-ior, we safe-ly may lean, And feel that our

Chorus. O Je-sus, my Sav-ior, in in-fin-ite love, Now send me thy

burden of sor-row oppressed,
Savior, to have them redressed.
worthy of grace from the Lord,
courage and strength are restored.

blessing of peace from a-bove.

3. What deep consolation the Savior imparts,
   To spirits wherein he abides as a guest!
   From those who receive him, he never departs,
   But gives his beloved both comfort and rest.

4. How empty the pleasures of earth do appear
   Compared to the riches of infinite love,
   That shine in the Savior of sinners so dear,
   How sweet to our spirits this rest from above!

Good News Comes O'er The Sea.

Moderato.

Words and Music by Rev. I. Baltzell, by per

1. Good news comes o'er the sea, And tells of vic - t'ry there; The
2. The glorious gos - pel light, In splendor shines to-day, Where
3. A - wake, the sun is high, The Master's call-ing you! Why

Duet.

heathen bow the knee, In humble, fervent pray'r; Long waited we to
naught but darkest night Fell on the heathen's way ; Brave Christians heard the
stand ye i - dle by ? There's work for you to do! Your treasures, pray'rs, and

hear The glorious tid-ings come, Proclaiming vic-t'ry there, Where
cry That came across the sea, "Come help us, ere we die, Come,
tears, Go, lay at Je - sus' feet; And soon we'll sing the song Of

Chorus. Lively.

darkness reigned alone. Re-joice, re-joice, Good news comes o'er the
help us to be free."
vic - tor-y complete. Rejoice, rejoice, rejoice, rejoice,

Repeat Chorus.

sea ; Re-joice, re-joice, Good news comes o'er the sea.
the sea ; Rejoice, rejoice, rejoice, rejoice,

H. B. H.

J. H. T.

1. "I know that my Redeemer lives," I feel his kindling love ; I'll bear the cross till
2. "I know that my Redeemer lives" To intercede for me ; And by his rich a-
3. "I know that my Redeemer lives," The Universal King ; Let all on earth and

Chorus.

I shall gain My crown in heav'n above.　　Hal-le - lu - - jah! Hal-le-
bounding grace I'm saved eternally.
　　all in heav'n To him their praises bring.　Hal-le-lu-jah evermore ! Hal-le-

lu - - jah! Je - sus stands and bids me, bids me come, Hal-le -
lu-jah ev - er-more! Je - sus stands and bids me come,　　Hal - le -

lu - - jah! Halle - lu - - jah! I am on my journey home.
lu-jah evermore! Halle-lu-jah evermore!

Only Waiting.

W. G. Irvin.   J. H. Fillmore.

1. I am waiting for the morning   Of the blessed day to dawn,
2. I am waiting, worn and weary   With the battle and the strife,
3. Waiting for the golden cit - y, Where the many mansions be ;

When the sor-row and the sad-ness   Of this wea-ry life are gone.
Hop-ing, when the war has ended,   To re-ceive a crown of life.
Listening for the happy welcome   Of my Sav-ior calling me.

Chorus.

I am wait - - ing, on-ly wait-ing,   Till this

I am waiting, waiting, waiting, only waiting, waiting, waiting, Till this

wea - - ry life is o'er,   On-ly wait - - ing

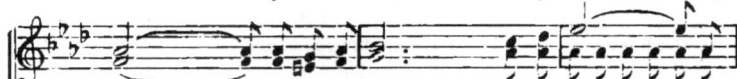

weary, weary, wea-ry life is o'er, life is o'er, Only waiting, waiting, waiting,

for my welcome   From my Savior on the oth - er shore.

May repeat pp.

for my welcome, for my welcome From my Savior on the other shore.

From "Songs of Glory," by per.

His Keeping Power

ANNIE RUDDICK.

T. B. WEAVER.

1. Sav-ior, fold me in thy arms, Keep me safe from earth's a-
2. Keep me hum - ble at thy feet, Always for thy use made
3. Knowest thou my pains and fears; Lord, thou se - est all my
4. Sav-ior, al - ways be my guide, While on life's un-ev-en

larms; Keep me washed in Je-sus blood— Keep me in the crimson
meet; May I, Sav - ior, find in thee, Re-fuge, fa - vor, lib-er-
tears; Lov-ing Sav - ior, meek and mild, Thou dost guide thy loving
tide; Guide me to the streets of gold, Safe-ly housed within thy

Chorus.

flood.
ty.
child.
fold. Sweet-ly saved! all hail to the Lamb! all glo-ry and

|1.
praise to Je-sus be giv'n,

|2.
praise to Jesus be giv'n!

Trusting In The Promise.

H. B. H.   E. S. LORENZ.

1. I have found re-pose for my wea-ry soul, Trusting in the promise of the
2. I will sing my song as the days go by, Trusting in the promise of the
3. Oh, the peace and joy of the life I live, Trusting in the promise of the

Savior; And a harbor safe when the billows roll, Trusting in the promise of the
Savior; And rejoice in hope, while I live or die, Trusting in the promise of the
Savior; Oh, the strength and grace only God can give. Trusting in the promise of the

Sav - ior. I will fear no foe in the deadly strife, Trusting in the promise of the
         I will bear my lot in the toil of life, Trusting in the promise of the
Sav - ior. I can smile at grief, and abide in pain, Trusting in the promise of the
         And the loss of all shall be highest gain, Trusting in the promise of the
Sav - ior. Who-so-ever will may be saved to-day, Trusting in the promise of the
         And begin to walk in the holy way, Trusting in the promise of the

Refrain.

1.   2.

Sav - ior,   Savior. Resting on His mighty arm forever, Never from his loving heart to

sev - er, I will rest by grace In his strong embrace, Trusting in the promise of the Savior.

From "Heavenly Carols," by per.

Seeking for Me.

From "Good Will," by per.

E. E. HASTY.

1. Je - sus, my Sav-ior, to Beth-le-hem came, Born in a man-ger to
2. Je - sus, my Sav-ior, on Cal - va-ry's tree, Paid the great debt, and my
3. Je - sus, my Sav-ior, the same as of old, While I did wan - der a-
4. Je - sus, my Sav-ior, shall come from on high, Sweet is the promise as

sorrow and shame; Oh, it was wonderful, blest be his name, Seeking for me, for
soul he set free; Oh, it was wonderful, how could it be? Dying for me, for
far from the fold, Gently and long he hath plead with my soul, Calling for me, for
wea-ry years fly; Oh, I shall see him descending the sky, Coming for me, for

for me......   for me......

me,   Seeking for me, Seeking for me, Seeking for me, Seeking for me;
me,   Dy-ing for me, Dying for me, Dying for me, Dying for me;
me,   Calling for me, Calling for me, Calling for me, Calling for me;
me,   Coming for me, Coming for me, Coming for me, Coming for me;

Oh, it was wonderful, blest be his name, Seeking for me, for me.
Oh, it was wonderful, how could it be? Dying for me, for me.
Gently and long he hath plead with my soul, Calling for me, for me.
Oh, I shall see him descending the sky, Coming for me, for me.

Have You Not A Word For Jesus?

From "Songs of Gratitude," by per.   J. H. FILLMORE.

1. { Have you not a word for Je-sus? Will the world his praise proclaim?
   { Who shall speak if ye are si - lent, Ye who know and ......
2. { He has spoken words of bless-ing, Par-don, peace and love to you,
   { Glo-rious hope and gracious comfort, Strong and tender, ...

Refrain.

love his name? Ye whom he hath called and chosen His own witnesses to be,
sweet and true? Does he hear you telling others Something of his love untold,

Will you tell your gracious Mas-ter, "Lord, we cannot speak for thee?"
O - verflow-ings of thanksgiv-ing For his mer-cies man-i - fold?

3. Have you not a word for Jesus? Some, perchance, while ye are dumb,
Wait and weary for your message, Hoping you will bid them come;
Never telling hidden sorrows, Ling'ring just outside the door.
Longing for your hand to lead them Into rest forevermore.

4. Yours may be the joy and honor Some poor ransomed souls to bring,
Jewels for the coronation Of your coming Lord and King;
Will you cast away the gladness, Thus your Master's joy to share,
All because a word for Jesus Seems too much for you to dare?

The Sun Of Righteousness.

1. As the rising sun disperses
   All the gloomy shades of night,
So the coming of the Savior
   Turns our darkness into light.
   Refrain
Sun of Glory! shine forever,
   In this lowly heart of mine;
Take away all sin and darkness;
   Fill me with thy love divine.

2. Light and life, and joy and beauty,
   Everywhere his coming brings;
Weep no longer, trembling mourner,
   There is healing in his wings.

3. Christ has come! My soul, receive him,
   Why one moment more delay?
He is ready, he is waiting
   All thy sins to wash away.

MRS. MARY F. MARSH.

My Spirit is Free.

W. A. S.   Rev. W. A. SPENCER, by per.

1. I fol-low the foot-steps of Je-sus, my Lord, His
2. A lep-er he found me, pol-lut-ed by sin, From
3. A cap-tive in woe to my pris-on of night The
4. Pro-claim it, 'tis done, full sal-va-tion is wrought For

Spir-it doth lead me a-long; I walk in the path-way made
which he a-lone can set free; He spake in His mer-cy, "I
Mas-ter hath o-pen'd the door; Shout a-loud of deliv'rance, ye
sin-ners from sor-row and woe; Sing a-loud of His grace who my

plain by His word, And He fills all my soul with this song.
will, be thou clean," And He in-stant-ly pu-ri-fied me.
an-gels of light, Praise His name, oh my soul, ev-er-more.
par-don has bought, "For His blood washes whit-er than snow."

Chorus.

Glo-ry to God! my spir-it is free, Glo-ry to God, He pu-ri-fies me! I'm

walking the thorn-path, but joyful I'll be While following Je-sus my Lord.

I Would Not Live Without Thee.

Mrs. Belle Towne. From "Good Will," by per. S. Wesley Martin.

1. I would not live without thee, Not a day, not a day. I need thy strength to
2. The world is full of sorrow, And of fears, and of fears; And many eyes are
3. The way is fraught with danger For us all, for us all; Oh, Savior, never
4. I'll fear no coming sorrow, Light will shine, light will shine. There'll come with ev'ry

help me, All the way, all the way; I would not dare to wander From thy
ever Shedding tears, shedding tears; And hearts are well nigh breaking With their
leave me, Lest I fall, lest I fall; When thou dost walk beside me, I am
morrow, Help di-vine, help divine; And when the journey's ended, Then I

side, from thy side. For storms and danger threaten Far and wide, far and wide.
woe, with their woe; And many vainly struggle Here below, here below.
strong, I am strong, To fight the many battles All a-long, all a-long.
know, then I know, To realms of endless glory I shall go, I shall go.

Chorus.

I would not live with-out thee, Dear Sav-ior, thou art mine;

Thy love doth make a heav-en, For me a world di-vine.

Hast Thou Heard Of Jesus?

Mrs. E. C. Ellsworth.　　　　　　　　　　　　　　　　J. H. T.

1. Hast thou heard of that won-der-ful Je-sus, Who dwelt among sin-ners, a
2. Hast thou heard of that won-der-ful Je-sus, Re - ject - ed by sinners of
3. Hast thou heard that this wonderful Je-sus, Dwells now with the low-ly in

God? Who in pu - ri-ty walked with the vil - est, Dis-
old? He is wait - ing to - day to be gra - cious, Yet
beart? With the hum - ble he walks in com-mun - ion, And

pens - ing his fa-vors a - broad?
slight - ed by numbers un-told.
grace he will free-ly im-part.

Chorus.

Oh, that won-der-ful, won-der-ful
Je - sus! He left the bright glory a - bove, On a
world in its sin and its ru - in, To pour out his in-fi-nite love.

There Is Joy In Heaven.

REV. H. B. HARTZLER.   J. H. T.

1. There is joy in heaven, where the angels dwell, And the gladsome notes of rejoicing swell,
2. There is joy in heaven, when the lost is found, And the golden streets with the news resound,
3. There is joy in heaven, that begins below, Where the tears of grief and repentance flow;

When the tidings come from the world below, That a soul is saved from eternal woe.
Till the tide of song like an ocean rolls Unto Him who died for the love of souls.
And the saints of God with the angels share In the praise that rings like an anthem there.

Chorus.

Beautiful song! Beautiful song! Beautiful song! Beautiful song of
Beautiful song! Beautiful song! Beautiful song! Beautiful

joy!   Ev'ry harp is at-tuned un - to the sound, And the angels
song of joy!

mp.   *cresc.*

re - joice that the lost is found, Beautiful song! Beautiful song of joy!

Song of joy, Beau-ti-ful song, hap-py song of joy!

Decide To-Night.

"How long halt ye?"—1 Kings xviii. 21.

Slow and with expression.   W. A. Spencer, by per.

1. Some go a-way from the house to-night, Pu - ri-fied from sin;
2. Some will go out from the house of pray'r, Hard - en'd by de - lay,
3. Some will go out from the house to-night, Full of trust in God,
4. Wait-ing a mo - ment more for thee, Je - sus still en - treats;

Chorus. *Go-ing a-way from Christ to-night, A-way from his lov-ing care;*

Fine.

Oth - ers re - ject the pre-cious light, And go a - way un - clean:
Yielding to Sa - tan's lur-ing snare, Will hope-less turn a - way:
Hap-py in heart, made pure and white, By Je - sus' pre-cious blood:
Soon will the knock-ing end - ed be, That now thy closed hearts beats:

Go - ing a - way from bless-ed light, To darkness and de-spair.

Lov - ing-ly still the Sav - ior stands, Plead-ing with thy heart;
Nev-er-more shall the Spir - it plead, At the bolt - ed door;
Go not a - way, poor wand'rer, stay Till thou too art free!
Stay, sin-ner, stay at Mer - cy's door, Seek the o - pen gate:

D. C. for Chorus.

Patiently knocks with his bleeding hands, Un-will-ing to de - part.
Now is the hour of thy soul's great need, 'Tis now or nev - er - more.
Walking with Christ life's hap-py way, Most bless - ed shalt thou be.
Sin-ner, de-cide lest hope be o'er, And thou shouldst be too late.

Jesus, Love Me Still.

E. A. H.   JNO. R. SWENEY

1. Oh, what utter weakness fills this soul of mine! How my fre-quent
2. Man-y are the fail-ures in my life I see; Man-y are the
3. Pi-ty me, dear Je-sus, if I sometimes fall; I among thy

stumblings wound thy heart di-vine!   Count me not un-wor-thy,
frail-ties cling-ing un-to me;   Yet, O precious Sav-ior,
ser-vants am the least of all,   Weak-est of the weak ones

:S: *Fine.*

Je-sus, keep me thine; Love me still, Je-sus, love me still.
smile complacently,   Love me still, Love and bless me still.
who up-on thee call;   Therefore, love me, Je-sus, love me still.

Precious Savior!   O, to love thee more!

Chorus.

Oh, what tender mercy! oh, what wondrous love! Oh, what rich compassion

D.S. :S:

hails me from above;   How can I but love thee, and thy grace adore!

From "The Garner," by per.

Draw Me Closer To Thee.

Mrs. E. W. Chapman.   J. H. T.

1. Clos-er to thee, my Father, draw me, I long for thine em-
2. Clos-er to thee, my Savior, draw me, Nor let me leave thee
3. Clos-er by thy sweet Spirit draw me, Till I am whol-ly

brace;   Clos-er within thine arms en-fold me, I seek a rest-ing
more;   Sigh-ing to feel thine arms a-round me, And all my wand'rings
thine;   Quicken, refine, and wash and cleanse me, Till pure my soul shall

Chorus.

place.   Clos - - er   with the cords of love,
o'er.
shine.   Clos-er, clos-er with the cords of love,

Draw   me   to thyself a-bove; Clos - - er
Draw me, draw me to thyself a - bove; Closer with the cords of love,

draw   me,   To   thy-self a - bove.
Draw me to thyself a-bove, Draw me to thy-self a - bove.

4

I Am Listening.

It is the voice of my beloved that knocketh, saying, Open to me.—Cant. 5: 2.

W. S. MARSHALL. W. S. MARSHALL.

1. Do you hear the Sav-ior call-ing, By the woo - ings of his
2. By his *Spir-it* he is woo-ing, Soft-ly draw-ing us to
3. By the *Word* of Truth he's speak-ing To the wand'ring, er-ring
4. In his *Prov-i - den-tial deal-ings*, E - ven in his stern de-

voice? Do you hear the ac-cents falling? Will you make the precious choice?
him, Thro' the day and night pur-su-ing, With his gen-tle voice to win.
ones; List! the voice the still-ness breaking! Hear the sweet and solemn tones!
crees, In the loudest thunders pealing, Or the murm'ring of the breeze.

Refrain.

I am list-'ning. Oh, I'm list-'ning Just to hear the ac-cents

Repeat softly.

fall; I am list-'ning. Oh, I'm list'ning To the Sav-ior's gentle call.

By permission.

Safe In Jesus.

"Abide in Me."—John 14: 4.

Rev. H. B. Hartzler.   J. H. T.

1. At the feet   of Je-sus ly-ing,   Once I prayed   in anguish
2. On his lov - ing breast re-clin-ing,   I shall fail   and fall no
3. With the fin - al con-flict near-ing,   I am free   from all a-

sore; Now his own right hand sustains me, With his strength I faint no more.
more; Lo, he whispers, "I am with thee, Till thy days of toil are o'er."
larm; Lo, the conqu'ror stands beside me; He will keep my soul from harm.

Chorus.

Safe in Je-sus   now a - bid-ing,   I can smile   at all my

foes; Safe in Je-sus,   safe in Je-sus,   O how sweet is my re-pose!

Jesus Is Passing This Way.

E. A. H.   J H. T.

1. Is there a sin-ner a - wait - ing   Mer-cy and pardon to - day?
2. Brother, the Master is wait - ing,   Waiting to free-ly for - give;
3. Yes, he is coming to bless you   While in contrition you bow;

Welcome the news that we bring him: "Jesus is passing this way!"
Why not this moment accept him, Trust in his grace and live?
Coming from sin to re-deem you, Read-y to save you now;

Coming in love and in mer - cy,   Pardon and peace to be-stow,
He is so tender and pre - cious,   He is so near you to - day;
Can you re-fuse the sal-va - tion   Je - sus is of-fer-ing here?

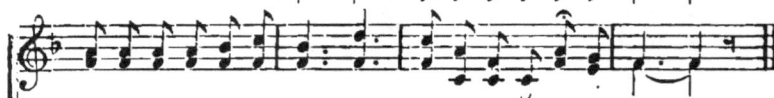

Coming to save the poor sin - ner   From his heart-anguish and woe.
O-pen your heart to receive him,   While he is passing this way.
O-pen your heart to ad-mit him,   While he is coming so   near.

Chorus.

Je-sus is passing this way...... To - day,........ to - day,
Jesus is passing this way, To-day, is passing to-day!

While he is near, O be-lieve him, O-pen your heart to receive him, For

Je-sus is passing this way, this way, Is passing this way to-day.

The Way, The Truth, The Life.

E. R. Latta.   J. H. T.

1. "I am the way," the Savior said; The paths of sin forsake;
Slumber no more in error's night, In . . . . . righteousness awake.
2. "I am the truth," the Savior said; In faith draw near to me;
He that believeth shall be saved, The . . . . truth shall make him free.
3. "I am the life," the Savior said. Your sins and sorrows leave;
Shun ye the path that leads to death; E - - - - ter-nal life receive.

Chorus.

I am the way, I am the way, I am the way, the truth, the life.

I am the way, I am the way, I am the way, the truth, the life.

54

"Pray Without Ceasing."

Words and Music by CHESTER E. POND, by per

1. My Lord and my Sav - ior, Cre - a - tor and King,
My soul is in rap - tures, Thou reign - est with - in,
2. How bril - liant my path - way when Thou art my Light,
How honored and glo - rious Thy tem - ple to be.
3. How sweet my com - mun - ion when low at Thy feet;
Now con - scious - ly feel - ing Thy Spir - it's con - trol.

Thy love and Thy glo-ry for-ev-er I'll sing;
To car-ry my burdens and . . . . cleanse me from sin.
How clear is my vis-ion when Thou art my Sight,
And know that Thou dwellest each . . . . moment in me.
Ful-fil-ing Thy will is my drink and my meat;
With joy I sur-render my . . . . bod-y and soul.

Chorus.

O help me re-mem-ber by night and by day, To "Pray with-out
ceas-ing," Thy word to o-bey! For noth-ing so pure and so
pre-cious to me, As se-cret and constant communion with Thee.

My Anchor Is Holding.

Mrs. E. W. Chapman.　　　　　　　　J. H. Tenney, by per.

"Which hope we have as an anchor of the soul." Heb. 6, 19.

1. Sweet Hope, the anc' or of my soul, En-ters with-in the vail;
2. My life's frail bark is of-ten tossed, High on the mountain waves
3. Fair Heaven's dome is just in view, Beau-ti-ful, gold-en land!

Rests in the Sa-viour's dy-ing love; Fears not the wild-est gale.
Steadfast and sure my an-chor holds, Firm on the Rock that saves.
Soon I shall reach its gate of pearl, Walk on his shin-ing strand.

CHORUS.

My an-chor is hold-ing, is hold-ing, With-in the vail; My

an-chor is hold-ing, is hold-ing, It will not fail.

The Shining City.

Theo. S. M. Tipton.   E. H. Bailey.

1. Far a - way, far away, ov-er the si - lent sea, Far off on that shining
2. O   Zi-on, blest Zion, it   stand - eth sure, Its beauties may not wax
3 Bright home of the blessed, it knoweth no night, It need-eth no moon nor

shore,   There stand-eth   a   cit - y,   we long   to be   With-
old;   The walls, they are all   of   the jas - per pure,   Its
sun;   The Lamb, in its midst, is   its   liv - ing light,   Its

Chorus.

in   it for - ev - er more.
streets of the glittering gold.   O! beau - ti - ful home, where the
tem - ple the Ho - ly One.

a tempo.

bright ones roam, Where they drink of the stream of life! We long to be

there, where they know no care, Where there cometh no sound of strife.

From the "International Lesson Hymnal" for 1879, by per.

'Neath Elim's Cooling Palms.

Rev. B. F. Bristow.   F. L. Bristow.

1. We are toil - ing on-ward, hand in hand, hand in hand, We are
2. By the swell - ing wa-ters, clear and sweet, clear and sweet, Aft-er
3. There will be no dark and drea-ry night, drea-ry night, We shall

toil - ing for the promised land; Come and join our weary pil-grim
toil - ing thro' the desert's heat, We shall rest our worn and wea-ry
rest for - ev - er from the fight; We shall dwell for - ev - er in the

band, pilgrim band, We shall rest 'neath Elim's cool-ing palms.
feet, wea-ry feet, We shall rest 'neath Elim's cool-ing palms.
light, in the light, We shall rest 'neath Elim's cool-ing palms.

Chorus.

{ Tho' the waves loud-ly roar, We shall pass safe-ly o'er. To the
{ By the clear sil - ver gleam Of the life - giv - ing stream, We shall

1.
bright happy shore of the blest, we shall rest;)
2.
) rest 'neath Elim's cooling palms.

From "Golden Gate," by per. of J. Church & Co., Cincinnati, O.

When We All Get Home.

E. A. H.   E. A. H.

1. We will sing the praise of Je - sus When we all get home, We will
2. All our tri - als will be ov - er, When we reach our home, All our
3. We will see our precious Savior When we all get home; We will

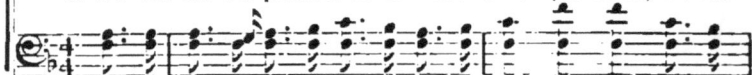

sing the praise of Jesus When we all get home, With millions round the throne, With the
trials will be ov-er, When we reach our home; How happy we will be, From all
see our precious Savior When we all get home ; His glory we shall see, And thro'

myriads of his own, We will make his glo-ry known When we all get home.
sin and sor-row free Thro' a long e-ter-ni-ty, In our heaven-ly home!
all e-ter - ni - ty, O how hap-py we shall be, In our heavenly home.

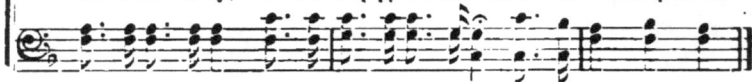

Chorus.

When we all get home ov - er there, ov - er there, When we

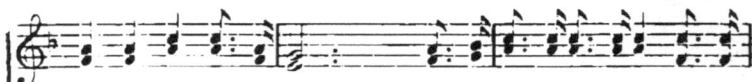

all get home, ov-er there, ov-er there, O how happy we will be When his

glo - ry we shall see, When we all get home, ov - er there, ov - er there.

Nearer The Cross.

Mrs. Valenstyne. Mrs. J. F. Knapp, by per.

1. Nearer the cross, my heart can say, I'm com-ing near - er;
Nearer the cross from day to day, I'm com-ing . . . .

near - er. { Nearer the cross where Je - sus died, }
{ Nearer the foun-tain's crimson tide, } Near-er my Sav-ior's

wound-ed side, I'm com-ing near - er, I'm com-ing near - er.

2. Nearer the Christian's mercy-seat,
Feasting my soul on manna sweet,
Stronger in faith, more clear I see,
Jesus who gave himself for me,
Nearer to him I still would be,
  Still coming nearer.

3. Nearer in prayer my hope aspires,
Deeper the love my soul desires,
Nearer the end of toil and care,
Nearer the joy I long to share,
Nearer the crown I soon shall wear,
  I'm coming nearer.

Oh, Leave Me Not Alone.

Words and Music by M. L. R., by per.

Softly. p

1. My life is filled with sad re-grets; No peace attends my way;
2. In-dul - gent God of love and power, To Thee for help I fly;
3. I know thou canst not let me go, Thy blood for me was shed;

f

Each day the sun in dark-ness sets, Oh, hear me, Lord, I pray.
Be with me at this solemn hour, And hear my con - trite sigh.
Now let me sink beneath its flow, And raise me from the dead.

m

Oh, let me not in dark-ness rove, But melt my heart of stone:
Re-new my heart and be my guide To Thy ce - les - tial throne,
And bid me stretch my withered arm To Thee, whose love is shown,

f

Ac-cept my faint attempts at love, And fix my heart on things a-bove;
Oh, let me see Thy wounded side; I come to Thee, the cru - ci-fied;
And grasp Thy mantle, with its charm, To take from death its dread a-larm,

p

"Come Ho - ly Spir - it, heavenly Dove," Oh, leave me not a - lone,
Lord con - de-scend to be my guide, Oh, leave me not a - lone,
And then, re-clin - ing on Thine arm, I shall not be a - lone,

"Come Ho-ly Spir - it, heavenly Dove," Oh, leave me not a - lone.

Wonderful Grace.

REV. W. H. BURRELL.

REV. I. BALTZELL, by per.

1 'Tis grace! 'tis grace! 'tis wonderful grace! This great salvation brings;
The soul de-liv - ered of its load, In

2. sweet - est rap - ture sings.

Chorus.

'Tis grace! . . . 'Tis
'Tis won-der-ful grace! 'Tis

grace! . . . grace! . . . 'Tis
wonder-ful grace, Wonderful, wonderful, wonderful grace! 'Tis

grace! . . . 'tis grace! . . .
won-der-ful grace! 'tis wonderful grace, Flowing still freely for me.

2. 'Tis grace! 'tis grace! 'tis wonderful grace!
Which saves the soul from sin;
The power of rising evil slays,
And reigns supreme within.

3. 'Tis grace! 'tis grace! 'tis wonderful grace!
Its streams are full and free;
Are flowing now for all the race,
They even flow to me.

There's Light Over There.

"For the Lord God giveth them light."—Rev. 20-5.

MRS. E. W. CHAPMAN.   J. H. T.

1. When the way seems long and drea - ry, And thy limbs are weak and
2. When the hours seem dark and lone - ly, Fill'd with grief and sor-row
3. Ev - er in his love a - bid - ing, Strong in faith and hope con-

wea - ry, Still pursue the path of right, "At evening time it shall be light."
on - ly, Then the watchword keep in sight, "At evening time it shall be light."
fid-ing, Keep in view the Mansions bright, "At evening time it shall be light."

Chorus.

There's light over there, over there, There's light over
Over there, over there, There's

there, The bliss of that beauti - ful place, Will all
light over there, The bliss of that beauti-ful

thoughts of thy sor-row ef - face, There's light over there, over
place, Will all thoughts of thy sorrow ef - face, There's

There's light ov - er there, ov - er there.

there,   There's light ov - er there, there's light ov - er there.
light ov - er there,   ov - er there,

ov - er there, ov - er there.

Come To Jesus.

E. R. LATTA.   J. H. T.

1. Come to Je-sus! he will save you, Tho' your sins as crimson glow;
   If you give your hearts to Je - sus,
2. Come to Je-sus! do not tar - ry; En-ter in at mercy's gate;
   O de-lay not till the mor - row,
3. Come to Je-sus, dy-ing sin - ner! Oth-er Sav-ior there is none;
   He will share with you his glory,

He will make them white as snow.
Lest thy coming be too late.   Come to Je - sus! Come to Je - sus!
When your pilgrimage is done.
Come, come to-day! Come, come to-day!

Come to Jesus! come to-day,
Come to Jesus! come, yes, come, come to-day!   Come to Jesus! come, come to-day!

64

Deliverance Will Come.

Arr. by Rev. W. McDonald, by per.

1. I saw a way-worn traveler in tattered garments clad,
And struggling up the mountain, It seemed that he was sad;
His back was laden heavy, His strength was almost gone,
Yet he shouted as he journeyed, De-liv-er-ance will come.

Cho.--Then palms of vic-to-ry, Crowns of glo-ry, Palms of vic-to-ry, I shall wear.

2. I saw him in the evening,
The sun was bending low,
Had overtopped the mountain
And reached the vale below:
He saw the golden city,
His everlasting home,
And shouted loud hosanna!
Deliverance will come.

3. While gazing on that city
Just o'er the narrow flood,
A band of holy angels
Came from the throne of God;
They bore him on their pinions,
Safe o'er the dashing foam,
And joined him in his triumph,—
Deliverance has come.

My Father's House.

ELLEN M. H. GATES. Furnished by MR. SANKEY. W. O. PERKINS, by per.

1. I am far a-way from my Father's house, And the years in-crease, The lights are dim in the banquet halls, The wreaths are withering

My Father's House.—CONCLUDED.

on the walls, And I long for peace. *Cho.*—I will rise and go to my

Father's house, And in his mercies will I rejoice, with heart and voice.

2 I have sought the best that the world could give,
As an idle guest,
My Father's house with its mansions fair,
Is the place for me, and my heart is there,
For my home is best.

3. O the doubts and fears of the changeful years;
They have vex'd my soul!
But safe forever and white and grand,
My Father's house like a rock will stand,
While the ages roll.

No Time For Jesus.

CHAS. H. GABRIEL.   J. H. T.

1. No time to give to Je-sus! O soul, what dost thou say?
Wilt thou not, for thy Sav-ior Give

Fine.

of thy time to-day? His pre-cious life a ran-som For thee he freely

D. C. for Cho.

gave: He left his throne in glo-ry Thy sin-ful soul to save.

2. No time to give to Jesus!
O thankless soul! why not?
Remember, by his mercy,
Thy precious soul was bought;

Canst thou not, from thy moments,
Find time to give to prayer?
In faithful vineyard-labor
Some moments for him spare?—*Cho.*

Satisfied.

REV. J. PARKER. *Dedicated to Mrs. E. Remmington.* MRS. JOSEPH F. KNAPP. by per.

1. I shall not want, Halle - lu - jah! The weakest are safe in His care,
   Lamb-like I repose in his bo - som,
2. I shall not want! O how oft - en He sendeth me help from a-bove;
   Men trust to themselves in providing.

He loves me I've nothing to fear.   I'm sat - is-fied, yes, sat - is-fied,
But I in his bounti-ful love.

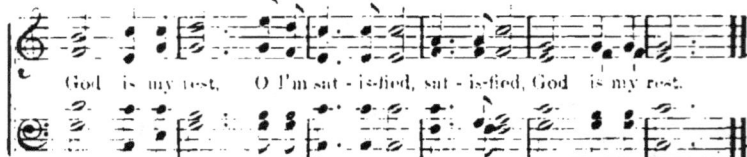

Chorus.

God is my rest,   O I'm sat - is-fied, sat - is-fied, God is my rest.

3. I shall not want! every murmur
   Is hushed by the sound of his voice;
   And though I may pass thro' the furnace,
   I lean on His arm and rejoice.

4. I shall not want! in the valley,
   Where shadows of death gather round,
   The morning of heaven will greet me,
   And gladness and glory abound.

No, Not Despairingly.

Andante.   From "Joy Bells," by per.   P. P. Bliss.

1. No, not de-spairingly Come I to thee;   No, not dis-tru-sting-ly

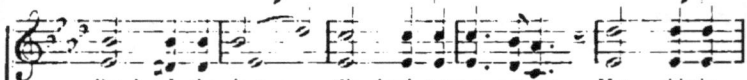

Bend I the knee;   Sin hath gone o - ver me,   Yet this is

No, Not Despairingly. Concluded.

still my plea, Je - sus hath died for me, Je - sus hath died.

2. Lord, I confess to thee
Sadly my sin;
Now, tell I all to thee,
All I have been;
Purge thou my sin away,
Wash thou my soul this day,
Take thou my sin away;
Lord, make me clean.

3. Faithful and just art thou.
Forgiving all;
Loving and kind art thou.
When sorrows call;
Lord, let the cleansing blood.
Let the dear healing flood.
Blood of the Lamb of God.
Pass o'er my soul.

I Shall Be Satisfied.

Dr. H. Bonar. Rev. T. C. Neal.

Moderato.

1. When I shall wake in that fair morn of morns, Af - ter whose dawn-ing
2. When I shall see thy glo - ry face to face, When in thine arms thou
3. When I shall meet with those that I have loved, Clasp in my ea - ger
4. When I shall gaze up - on the face of him Who for me died, with

never night returns, And with whose glory day eternal burns, I shall be sat-is-fied.
wilt thy child embrace, When thou shalt open all thy stores of grace, I shall be satisfied.
arms the long removed, And find how faithful thou to me hast proved, I shall be satisfied.
eye no longer dim, And praise him with the everlasting hymn, I shall be sat-is-fied.

Chorus. rit.

I shall be sat - is-fied, I shall be sat-is-fied, I shall be sat-is-fied, By and by.

From "Jasper and Gold," by per.

Tenderly Lead Me.

JNO. R. SWENEY.

1. Oh, lead me to Je - sus, I'm tired of my sin, And wea - ry with
2. Oh, lead me to Je - sus, I know he is love, To save erring
3. Oh, lead me to Je - sus, Oh, show me the way; My soul in its

fighting Po - lu - tion with-in; In mer - cy now lead me Where
children He came from a - bove; He sure - ly will heal me And
blindness Has wander'd a - stray; Then take me to Je-sus, So

I will find peace, And where all my sor-rows For-ev - er will cease.
par - don my sin, Then gra - ciously fill me With comfort with-in.
pre - cious is he, The dear lov ing Sav - ior Who suffer'd for me.

Chorus.

Oh, lead me so gen - tly, So gen - tly to Je-sus,
Lead me, oh, lead me so gently to Jesus, So gently, oh, lead me so gently to Jesus,

Ten - der - ly lead me a - way un - to him;
Tenderly, tenderly lead me, oh, lead me, Tenderly lead me away unto him;

From "Goodly Pearls," by per.

Tenderly Lead Me.—CONCLUDED.

For I am so wea - ry, so lone - ly and
For I'm so wea-ry, so lone-ly and dreary, For I am so wea-ry, with

drea - ry, With bearing my bur - den of sin.
out him so dreary, With bearing my bur-den, My bur - den of sin.

We Are Singing.

CHAS. H. GABRIEL. From S. S. Scholars Quarterly, by per. P. P. BLISS.

1. We are sing-ing, praises bringing, To our Sav-ior to - day,
For his kindness in our blindness,   Leading

Chorus.

safe-ly al - way. Hal-le - lu -jah! halle-lu-jah! Roll the chorus

a - long; Christ and glory, wondrous story! Is the theme of our song.

2. Care and trials, self denials
Meet we day after day ;
But so sweetly and completely
Jesus drives them away.

3. Brother, love him, come and prove him,
Your Redeemer and King,
He'll receive you and relieve you,
Hallelujah then sing.

70

Down At The Cross.

E. A. H. From "Dew of Hermon," by per. JOHN R. SWENEY.

1. Down at the cross where the Savior died, Down where for cleansing from
D. C. for Cho. There to my heart was the . . . .

sin I cried, } blood ap-plied, Glory, glo - ry, glory to his name.

Chorus. D. C.

Down at the cross, down at the cross, Down at the cross where Jesus died,

2. I am so wondrously saved from sin ;
Jesus so sweetly abides within,
Saves me each moment, and keeps me clean ;
Glory, glory, glory to his name!

3. Come to this fountain, so rich and sweet ;
Humble your soul at the Savior's feet;
Plunge in to-day, and be made complete,
And give glory, glory to his name!

I Shall Be Whiter Than Snow.

E. A. H. J. H. T.

1. Thy grace, O my Sav-ior, can reach ev - en me! I know that, if
2. My soul is all weakness, my heart is un-clean, But thy precious
3. I'll doubt thee no long-er, this mo-ment I'll go, And wash in the

washed in thy blood, I shall be Cho. Whit-er than snow, yes, whit-er than
blood can redeem from all sin.
blood that makes whiter than snow.

snow, If washed in that foun-tain I shall be whit-er than snow.

Why Don't You Receive Him?

E. A. H.   E. A. H.

1. O tarry no longer, my brother, But turn from your sins away;
   Come, bow at the feet of the Savior, And . . . .
2. While humbled in deepest contrition, In tears at his feet you bow,
   The Savior is ready and willing, And . . . .
3. He offers the gift of sal-va-tion, He waits for your promised vow,
   He brings you a free and full pardon, O . . . .

Chorus.

give him your heart to-day ! { Brother, why don't you believe him? }
wait-ing to save you now. { Brother, why don't you receive him? }
brother, receive him now !

Je - sus......... is wait-ing......... He's waiting to save you now.
Je - sus is waiting, he's waiting to day.

I Love The Name Of Jesus.

Words and music by W. T. GIFFE, by per

1. I love the name of Je - sus, I love the name of Je-sus, I love the name of
For Je - sus loves the sinner, For Jesus loves the sinner, For Jesus loves the

|1.
Je - sus, That name the an-gels sing;
|2.
did sal-va - tion bring.

sin - ner And . . . .

Chorus.

I love............... I love............... I

I love the name of Je - sus, I love the name of Je - sus, I

|1.
love the name of Je - sus;
|2.
love his pre-cious name.

2. He has a place in heaven,
Just by the great white throne;
'Tis for his faithful children,
When Jesus takes them home.

3. We're coming, blessed Savior,
With happy hearts and free;
Stretch out Thine arms and take us,
Thy children, Lord, to Thee.

Enough For Me.

E. A. H.   E. A. H.

1. O love sur-pass-ing knowledge! O grace so full and free!   I

Enough for Me—CONCLUDED.

Fine.

know that Je - sus saves me, And that's enough for me!

know that Je - sus saves me, And that's enough for me!

Refrain. D.S.

And that's enough for me! And that's enough for me! I

2. O wonderful salvation!
From sin he makes me free!
I feel the sweet assurance,
And that's enough for me!

3. O blood of Christ so precious,
Poured out on Calvary!
I feel its cleansing power,
And that's enough for me!

"Into Thy Hands, O Lord."

SUSAN J. ADAMS. J. H. T.

1. In - to Thy hands, O Lord, My-self I give, With all my cares and
2. All I have ev - er been Or hope to be; My hoarded gains, my
3. I would no longer stand An i - dler here, Thy work I would be
4. Thou knowest all my need, Bet-ter than I; Quicken my weak en-

tri - als, And weary self-denials, Long as I live, Long as I live.
losses, My triumphs and my crosses, I bring to Thee, I bring to Thee.
do - ing, Daily my toil renewing, Till Thou ap-pear, Till Thou ap-pear.
deav-or, That I may love Thee ever, Un-til I die, Un - til I die.

At Evening Time It Shall Be Light.

From the "International Lesson Hymnal," for 1879, by per.

Mrs. M. E. Cox.   W. O. Perkins.

1. If in-stead of high-est path-ways, Low-ly ones on
2. Aft-er earn-est, strong en-deav-or, Pa-tient toil for

earth you tread, Do not deem your life a fail-ure, Nor let
ma-ny years, If your wea-ry, faith-ful la-bor Al-most

Chorus.

use-less tears be shed; { Lean on Je - sus, look to heav-en,
with-out fruit ap-pears, { Sweet the promise that is giv-en,

||1. ||2.

Tho' all a-round be dark as night; }
At evening . . . .   time it shall be light.

O Take Me As I Am.

E. H. H.

1. Je-sus, my Lord, to thee I cry, Unless Thou help me, I must die: Oh,
2. Helpless I am, and full of guilt, But yet for me Thy blood was spilt, And
3. No pre-pa-ra-tion can I make, My best resolves I on-ly break, Yet

Cho. I lin-ger at the mercy seat; Behold me, Savior, at thy feet! Thy

bring thy free sal - va - tion nigh, And take me as I am!
Thou canst make me what Thou wilt, But take me as I am!
save me for Thine own Name's sake, And take me as I am!

work in me be - gin, complete; O take me as I am!

The Sinner's Friend.

J. G.   From "S. S. Scholars' Quarterly, by per.   JOSEPH GARRISON.

1. Tho' thy way seems dark and drea - ry, Gloomy doubts thy
There is one who waits to cheer thee, One who . . . .
2. Is thy heart, by sin pol - lut - ed, Sink-ing down in
There is one whose blood will cleanse it, Whit-er . . . .
3. Does thy con - science oft con-demn thee? Is there an - guish
There is one, sweet peace can give thee, He can . . . .

D. C. Come, oh, come, ob - tain his fa - vor, And be . . . .

steps at - tend: } is the sin-ner's friend. It is Je - sus
end-less woe? } than the driv-en snow.
in thy breast? } give thee per-fect rest.

rec - on - ciled to God.

D. C.

thy dear Sav - ior, He who bought thee with his blood;

Persuaded.

E. A. H.   E. A. H

1. God in his mer - cy Calls un - to me, And I'm ful - ly per-
2. Je - sus en-treats me So ten-der - ly, And I'm ful - ly per-
3. Heav - en now off - ers Par - don to me, And I'm ful - ly per-

sund - ed A Christ-ian to be.
sund - ed A Chris-tian to be.
sund - ed A Chris-tian to be.

Refrain.

I'm ful - ly persuad - ed,

Ful - ly per-suad-ed, Ful - ly per-suad-ed A Christian to be.

"This I Did For Thee."

A. B. B.   A. B. Bragdon.

1. I left my glorious home on high, I left my Father's
2. And thro' the earth for many a day My wea - ry feet have
3. Up - on my head a crown of thorns, A spear-wound in my
4. Oh! give to me thy wayward heart, The days that yet re-

"This I Did For Thee."—CONCLUDED.

throne, I came to earth to bleed and die, And for thy sins a-
trod, That I might lead thee to the way, And bring thee home to
side, With hands and feet all rent and torn Up - on the cross I
main, And from my precepts ne'er depart, Nor let me die in

tone; I gave up Heaven, O sinner, for thee,—What hast thou done for me?
God; I bore the cross, O sinner, for thee,—What hast thou done for me?
died; I gave my life, O sinner, for thee,—What hast thou done for me?
vain; Give thou thyself, O sinner, to me, Since I have died for thee.

Jesus, Lead The Way.

Arr. by J. H. T.

1 Je-sus, lead the way. So we shall not stray { From the path while
But shall follow

2. Should our tare be hard, Be thou our reward; { Should our days be
And our burdens

3. Should the tempters darts Vex and wound our hearts, { Then in all our
Grant us patience,

Rit.   *Rall.*

here abiding, } Lead us by the hand. To that better land.
thy safe guiding; }
very drea-ry, } Lead us by the hand, To that better land.
very wea-ry, }
woe and weakness, } Lead us by the hand, To that better land.
grant us meekness; }

Nothing But The Blood Of Jesus.

R. L. — R. LOWRY, by per.

1. What can wash a - way my sin? Nothing but the blood of Je - sus; }
   What can make me whole a - gain? Nothing but the blood of Je - sus }
2. For my cleansing this I see— Nothing but the blood of Je - sus;
   For my par - don this my plea— Nothing but the blood of Je - sus. }

Chorus.

Oh, pre-cious is the flow That makes me white as snow;

No oth-er fount I know, Nothing but the blood of Je - sus.

3. Nothing can for sin atone,
   Nothing but the blood of Jesus;
   Naught of good that I have done,
   Nothing but the blood of Jesus.

4. This is all my hope and peace—
   Nothing but the blood of Jesus;
   This is all my righteousness —
   Nothing but the blood of Jesus.

Christ's Cross.

REV. J. H. BRALE. — E. A. H.

1. O Sav - ior di - vine, I would lov - ing - ly twine These hands close a-
   As, nailed to the tree, thou dost suf - fer for me, And all that sal-
2. Rich garlands I bring to the cross of my King, And close to its
   I'd gaze on his face, so a - bound-ing in grace, And no more de-
3. For Christ and his cross I count all things but loss! Tho' wild-ly my
   Yet anchored to Thee in life's storm-i - est sea, A re - fuge I

Christ's Cross.—CONCLUDED.

bout that dear per - son of thine,
va - tion to me may be free.
foot I for - ev - er would cling;
part from that heav - en - ly place.
bark on the bil - lows may toss,
know thou for - ev - er wilt be.

I'll trust my Redeem
I'll love him for - ev-

|1.

er, I'll praise and a - dore him, }

|2.

ev - er. A - men!
er and

This Fountain Cleanses from All Sin.

1. The blood that flowed from Cal - va - ry, From all my
2. O won - der - ful sal - va - tion this! Un - meas - ured
3. With joy I tell to oth - ers round What depths of

Cho. This foun - tain cleans - es from all sin, And ev - ery

sins now cleans - es me, And I praise my Redeem - er, my
wealth of love and peace! I will praise my Re - deem - er, my
mer - cy I have found; And I praise my Re - deem - er, my

one may now plunge in; There's a foun - tain, a foun - tain of

soul is free, For the blood now cleans - es me.
soul is free, For the blood now cleans - es me.
soul is free, For the blood now cleans - es me.

wa - ter and blood, Ev - er flow - ing for you and for me.

Nearer to Me.

Elisha A. Hoffman. William A. Galpin.

1. Draw near, O Christ, to me, Near - er to me, Un - worth-y and un-clean
2. Draw near, O Christ, to me, Near - er to me, My soul with strong desire
3. Draw near, O Christ, to me, Near - er to me, Let all thy wealth of love

Though I may be; Come with thy quick'ning grace, Show me thy
Burns aft - er thee; Let me thy joys par - take, Come ere my
Fall up - on me; Touch ev - ery se - cret sin, Wash me, and

smil-ing face, Draw near this hal - lowed place, Draw near to me.
spir - it break, For thy sweet mer - cy's sake, Draw near to me.
make me clean, Let noth-ing stand between My heart and thee.

Death and Eternity.

Words and Music by Chas. H. Gabriel, by per.

Feelingly.

1. Coming when the day is bright, Coming in the si-lent night, Coming at the morning
2. Coming to the gay and proud, Coming with a snow-white shroud, Coming to the gray head
3. Coming with unhindered sway, Coming every fleet-ing day, Coming to the young and
4. Coming to the sin-ful one, Coming when our life is done, Gath'ring to the judgment

p Slow ad lib. *Echo.*

light. Coming, coming, death and e - ter - ni-ty, e-ter-ni-ty.
bowed, Coming, coming, death and e - ter - ni-ty, e-ter-ni-ty.
gay. Coming, coming, death and e - ter - ni-ty, e-ter-ni-ty.
Throne, Coming, coming, death and e - ter - ni-ty, e-ter-ni-ty.

Room For Jesus.

REV. T. J. SHELTON.

J. H. T.

1. Je - sus, I have room for thee, In my hum - ble dwell - ing;
2. Room with-in my heart for thee, Life's e - ter - nal foun - tain!
3. Room with-in my heart for thee, Suff'r - er in the gar - den!

Come to me a wel-come guest, All my sins ex - pell - ing
Room for Christ who bore the cross, Up to Calv' - ry's moun - tain.
If thou bring thy peace to me, If thou seal my par - don.

Fine.

D.S. Come and seal me with thy love, And be - stow thy fa - vor.

Chorus.

D.S.

Room for thee, room for thee, Pre - cious Lord and Sav - ior!

The Better Day Coming On.

M. L. ROSEVALLEY, by per.

1. My Je - sus, I love thee! I know thou art
My gra - cious Re - deem - er, my Sav - ior art

Chorus. There's a bet - ter day, there's a crowning day, There's a bet - ter day com - ing
Coming on, Coming on, Coming on, com - ing

mine, For thee all the pleas - ures of sin I re - sign;
thou. If ev - er I lov'd thee, my Je - sus, 'tis now.

on, There's a bet-ter day, there's a crowning day, There's a better day coming on.
on, There's a bet-ter day, there's a crowning day, There's a better day coming on.

2 I love thee because thou hast first loved me, 3. In mansions of glory, or heavenly delight,
And purchased my pardon, being nailed to the tree; I'll ever adore thee in regions of light;
I love thee for wearing the thorns on thy brow, And sing with a glittering crown on my brow,
If ever I loved thee, my Jesus, 'tis now.— If ever I loved thee, my Jesus, 'tis now.

82

DUKE STREET. L. M.   JOHN HATTON.

CHEMUNG. L. M.   By per. of A. N. JOHNSON.

WINDHAM. L. M.   DANIEL READ.

LUTON. L. M.   REV. GEORGE BURDER.

1

JUST as I am, without one plea,
But that thy blood was shed for me,
And that thou bid'st me come to thee,
O Lamb of God! I come, I come!

Just as I am, and waiting not
To rid my soul of one dark blot,
To thee, whose blood can cleanse each spot
O Lamb of God! I come, I come!

Just as I am; thou wilt receive,
Wilt welcome, pardon, cleanse, relieve;
Because thy promise I believe,
O Lamb of God! I come, I come!

2.

OH, take my fevered hands in thine,
And keep me Master, nearer thee,
Walking above the things of time,
In closest fellowship with thee.

Calm in thy secret presence, Lord,
I rest this weary soul of mine,
Feed on the fullness of thy word,
And die to all the things of time;

Such be my path while dwelling here,
One long, close, upward path with thee;
Until, past every doubt and fear,
Thy face in light above I see.

3.

O GOD, forgive the years and years
Of worldly pride and hopes and fears;
Forgive, and blot them from thy book,
The sins on which I mourn to look.

Forgive the lack of service done
For thee, thro' life, from life begun;
Forgive the vain desire to be
All else but that desired by thee.

Forgive the love of human praise,
The first false step in crooked ways,
The voice of evil and the night,
The heart close shut against the light.

Forgive the love that could endure
No cost to bless the sad and poor;
Forgive, and give me grace to see
The life laid down in love for me.

4.

WHEN I survey the wondrous cross
On which the Prince of glory died,
My richest gain I count but loss,
And pour contempt on all my pride.

See, from his head, his hands, his feet,
Sorrow and love flow mingled down;
Did e'er such love and sorrow meet,
Or thorns compose so rich a crown?

Were the whole realm of nature mine,
That were a present far too small;
Love so amazing, so divine,
Demands my soul, my life, my all!

5.

LORD, I am thine, entirely thine,
Purchased and saved by blood divine;
With full consent thine I would be,
And own thy sov'reign right in me.

Thine would I live, thine would I die;
Be thine through all eternity;
The vow is past, beyond repeal,
And now I set the solemn seal.

Here, at that cross where flows the blood
That bought my guilty soul for God,
Thee, my new Master, now I call,
And consecrate to thee my all.

6.

COME, Saviour, Jesus, from above,
Assist me with thy heavenly grace;
Empty my heart of earthly love,
And for thyself prepare the place.

O let thy sacred presence fill,
And set my longing spirit free;
Which pants to have no other will,
But day and night to feast on thee.

Henceforth may no profane delight
Divide this consecrated soul;
Possess it thou, who hast the right,
As Lord and Master of the whole.

7.

WITH tearful eyes I look around,
Life seems a dark and stormy sea;
Yet 'midst the gloom I hear a sound,
A heavenly whisper, "Come to me."

It tells me of a place of rest—
It tells me where my soul may flee;
Oh! to the weary, faint, oppressed,
How sweet the bidding, "Come to me."

O voice of mercy! voice of love!
In conflict, grief and agony,
Support me, cheer me from above!
And gently whisper, "Come to me."

8.

SHOW pity, Lord, O Lord forgive!
Let a repenting rebel live;
Are not thy mercies large and free?
May not a sinner trust in thee?

My crimes are great, but can't surpass
The power and glory of thy grace;
Great God, thy nature hath no bound,
So let thy pardoning love be found.

Oh wash my soul from every sin,
And make my guilty conscience clean;
Here on my heart the burden lies,
And past offenses pain mine eyes.

Yet save a trembling sinner, Lord,
Whose hope still hov'ring round thy word,
Would light on some sweet promise there,
Some sure support against despair.

9.

O THAT my load of sin were gone;
O that I could at last submit
At Jesus' feet to lay it down—
To lay my soul at Jesus' feet.

Rest for my soul I long to find;
Saviour of all, if mine thou art,
Give me thy meek and lowly mind,
And stamp thine image on my heart.

Break off the yoke of inbred sin,
And fully set my spirit free;
I cannot rest till pure within,—
Till I am wholly lost in thee.

84

DEVOTION. L. M. — Rev. D. S. Anderson.

FOREST. L. M. — Chapin.

HURSLEY. L. M. — Peter Ritter, Arr. by William Henry Monk.

ORIE. L. M. — E. A. Hoffman.

1.

O, BEULAH Land! Fair Beulah Land!
   Upon the shore of earth I stand,
And look across the narrow sea
That seperates yon Heaven from me.

O, Beulah Land, bright Beulah Land!
I feel my raptured soul expand
As I, with eager faith, behold
Yon walls of jasper, gates of gold.

O, Beulah Land! sweet vale of peace,
Whose very air is full of bliss, .
I linger in thy bowers of prayer,
The fragrance of God's love is there.

2.

I THIRST, thou wounded Lamb of God,
   To wash me in thy cleansing blood:
To dwell within thy wounds: then pain
Is sweet, and life or death is gain.

Take my poor heart, and let it be
Forever closed to all but thee:
Seal thou my breast, and let me wear
That pledge of love forever there.

3.

FROM every stormy wind that blows,
   From every swelling tide of woes,
There is a calm, a sure retreat;
'Tis found beneath the mercy-seat.

There is a place where Jesus sheds
The oil of gladness on our heads—
A place than all besides more sweet;
It is the blood bought mercy-seat.

There, there on eagle wings we soar,
And sin and sense molest no more;
And heaven comes down our souls to greet,
And glory crowns the mercy-seat.

4.

JESUS! and shall it ever be,
   A mortal man ashamed of thee!
Ashamed of thee, whom angels praise,
Whose glories shine through endless days!

Ashamed of Jesus, that dear friend,
On whom my hopes of heaven depend!
No, when I blush, be this my shame,
That I no more revere his name.

Ashamed of Jesus! yes, I may,
When I've no guilt to wash away,
No tears to wipe, no good to crave,
No fears to quell, no soul to save.

5.

SAY, sinner! hath a voice within,
   Oft whispered to thy secret soul,
Urged thee to leave the ways of sin,
And yield thy heart to God's control?

Sinner, it was a heavenly voice,—
   It was the Spirit's gracious call;
It bade thee make the better choice,
   And haste to seek in Christ thine all.

Spurn not the call to life and light;
   Regard, in time, the warning kind;
That call thou mayst not always slight,
   And yet the gate of mercy find.

6.

JESUS, a word, a look from thee,
   Can turn my heart, and make it clean,
Purge out the inbred leprosy,
   And save me from my bosom sin.

My heart, which now to thee I raise,
   I know thou canst this moment cleanse,
The deepest stains of sin efface,
   And drive the evil spirit hence.

Be it according to thy word;
   Accomplish now thy work in me;
And let my soul, to health restored,
Devote its deathless powers to thee.

7.

O LORD, thy sovereign aid impart,
   And guard the gift thyself hast given:
My portion thou, my treasure art,
   My life, and happiness, and heaven.

Would aught on earth my wishes share?
   Though dear as life the idol be,
The idol from my breast I'll tear,
   Resolved to seek my all in thee.

Whate'er I fondly counted mine,
   To thee, my Lord, I here restore;
Gladly I all to thee resign;
   Give me thyself, I ask no more.

8.

COME, Holy Spirit! calm my mind,
   And fit me to approach my God;
Remove each vain, each worldly thought,
   And lead me to thy blest abode.

Hast thou imparted to my soul,
   A living spark of holy fire?
Oh! kindle now the sacred flame;
   Make me to turn with pure desire.

A brighter faith and hope impart,
   And let me now my Saviour see;
Oh! soothe and cheer my burdened heart,
   And bid my spirit rest in thee.

9.

AWAKE, my soul, in joyful lays,
   And sing thy great Redeemer's praise;
He justly claims a song from thee,
His loving kindness oh, how free!

He saw me ruined in the fall,
Yet loved me notwithstanding all;
He saved me from my lost estate,
His loving kindness, oh, how great!

Often I feel my sinful heart
Prone from my Saviour to depart;
But, though I oft have him forgot,
His loving kindness changes not.

Soon shall I pass the gloomy vale,
Soon all my mortal powers must fail;
Oh, may my last expiring breath
His loving kindness sing in death.

10.

O, THOU, to whose all-searching sight
   The darkness shineth as the light,
Search, prove my heart, it pants for thee;
Oh, burst these bonds, and set it free!

Wash out its stains, refine its dross,
Nail my affections to the cross;
Hallow each thought, let all within
Be clean, as thou, my Lord, art clean.

CORONATION. C. M. OLIVER HOLDEN.

CRESSEY. C. M. J. H. TENNEY, by per.

ARLINGTON. C. M. DR. ARNE.

AVON. C. M. Scottish Tune.

DUNDEE. C. M. G. FRANC.

WARWICK. C. M. S. STANLEY.

1.

VAIN man, thy fond pursuits forbear—
Repent—thy end is nigh!
Death, at the farthest, can't be far,
Oh, think—before thou die!

Reflect—thou hast a soul to save,
Thy sins—how high they mount!
What are thy hopes beyond the grave—
How stands that dread account?

To-day the Gospel calls, to-day,
Sinner, it speaks to you;
Let every one forsake his way,
And mercy will ensue.

2.

RETURN, O wanderer, return,
And seek thy Father's face;
Those new desires which in thee burn,
Were kindled by his grace.

Return, O wanderer, return;
Thy Saviour bids thee live:
Come to his cross, and, grateful, learn
How freely he'll forgive.

Return, O wanderer, return;
Regain thy long-sought rest:
The Saviour's melting mercies yearn
To clasp thee to his breast.

3.

FOREVER here my rest shall be,
Close to thy bleeding side;
This all my hope, and all my plea,
For me the Saviour died!

My dying Saviour, and my God,
Fountain for guilt and sin,
Sprinkle me ever with thy blood,
And cleanse, and keep me clean.

Wash me, and make me thus thine own;
Wash me, and mine thou art
Wash me, but not my feet alone,
My hands, my head, my heart.

Th' atonement of thy blood apply,
Till faith to sight improve;
Till hope in full fruition die,
And all my soul be love.

4.

WHEN I can read my title clear
To mansions in the skies,
I'll bid farewell to every fear,
And wipe my weeping eyes.

Cho.—We will stand the storm,
We will anchor by and by.

Let cares like a wild deluge come,
And storms of sorrow fall,
May I but safely reach my home,
My God, my heaven, my all!

There shall I bathe my weary soul
In seas of heavenly rest,
And not a wave of trouble roll
Across my peaceful breast.

5.

WHEN all thy mercies, O my God,
My rising soul surveys,
Transported with the view, I'm lost
In wonder, love, and praise.

O how can words with equal warmth
The gratitude declare,
That glows within my ravished heart?
But thou canst read it there.

Through all eternity to thee
A grateful song I'll raise;
But O, eternity's too short
To utter all thy praise.

6.

AM I a soldier of the cross,—
A foll'wer of the Lamb,—
And shall I fear to own his cause,
Or blush to speak his name?

Are there no foes for me to face?
Must I not stem the flood?
Is this vile world a friend to grace,
To help me on to God?

Sure I must fight if I would reign;
Increase my courage, Lord!
I'll bear the toil, endure the pain,
Supported by thy word.

7.

ALAS! and did my Saviour bleed?
And did my Sovereign die?
Would he devote that sacred head
For such a worm as I?

Was it for crimes that I have done,
He groaned upon the tree?
Amazing pity! grace unknown?
And love beyond degree!

But drops of grief can ne'er repay
The debt of love I owe;
Here, Lord, I give myself away,
'Tis all that I can do.

8.

DEAR Father, to thy mercy-seat
My soul for shelter flies:
'Tis here I find a safe retreat
When storms and tempests rise.

My cheerful hope can never die,
If thou, my God, art near;
Thy grace can raise my comforts high,
And banish every fear.

Oh, never let my soul remove
From this divine retreat!
Still let me trust thy power and love,
And dwell beneath thy feet.

9.

ALL hail the power of Jesus' name,
Let angels prostrate fall;
Bring forth the royal diadem,
And crown him—Lord of all.

Let high-born seraphs tune the lyre,
And as they tune it, fall
Before his face, who tunes their choir,
And crown him—Lord of all.

Ye seed of Israel's chosen race,
Ye ransomed of the fall:
Hail him who saves you by his grace,
And crown him—Lord of all.

Sinners! whose love can ne'er forgot,
The wormwood and the gall,
Go, spread your trophies at his feet,
And crown him—Lord of all.

88

CHRISTMAS. C. M.   GEORGE FREDERICK HANDEL.

EMMONS. C. M.   German Melody.

MELODY. C. M.   AARON CHAPIN.

MEAR. C. M.   Welsh Air.

ST. BERNARD. C. M.   LONDON TUNE BOOK.

1.

OH, for a closer walk with God,
  A calm and heavenly frame;
A light to shine upon the road
That leads me to the Lamb.

Where is the blessedness I knew,
  When first I saw the Lord?
Where is the soul-refreshing view
  Of Jesus and his word?

Return, O, holy Dove, return,
  Sweet messenger of rest
I hate the sins that made thee mourn,
  And drove thee from my breast.

The dearest idol I have known,
  Whate'er that idol be,
Help me to tear it from thy throne,
  And worship only thee.

2.

COME, Holy Spirit, heavenly Dove,
  With all thy quick'ning powers;
Kindle a flame of sacred love
  In these cold hearts of ours.

Dear Lord! and shall we ever live
  At this poor dying rate;
Our love so faint, so cold to thee,
  And thine to us so great?

Come, Holy Spirit, heavenly Dove,
  With all thy quick'ning powers;
Come shed abroad a Saviour's love,
  And that shall kindle ours.

3.

OH, for a faith that will not shrink,
  Though pressed by every foe,
That will not tremble on the brink
  Of any earthly woe;

That will not murmur or complain
  Beneath the chast'ning rod,
But in the hour of grief or pain
  Will lean upon its God;—

Lord, give us such a faith as this,
  And then, whate'er may come,
We'll taste e'en here, the hallowed bliss
  Of an eternal home.

4.

O, FOR a heart to praise my God,
  A heart from sin set free;
A heart that always feels thy blood,
  So freely spilt for me!

A heart resign'd, submissive, meek,
  My great Redeemer's throne;
Where only Christ is heard to speak,—
  Where Jesus reigns alone.

A heart in every thought renew'd,
  And full of love Divine;
Perfect, and right, and pure, and good,
  A copy, Lord, of thine.

Thy nature, gracious Lord, impart;
  Come quickly from above;
Write thy new name upon my heart—
  Thy new, best name of Love.

5.

FATHER, I stretch my hands to thee,
  No other help I know;
If thou withdraw thyself from me,
  Ah, whither shall I go?

Cho.—Help me, dear Saviour, thee to own,
  And ever faithful be;
And when thou sittest on thy throne,
  O Lord, remember me.

What did thine only Son endure,
  Before I drew my breath!
What pain, what labor, to secure
  My soul from endless death!

Author of faith, to thee I lift
  My weary, longing eyes:
Oh, let me now receive that gift,
  My soul without it dies.

6.

JESUS, thine all-victorious love
  Shed in my heart abroad,
Then shall my feet no longer rove,
  Rooted and fix'd in God.

O, that in me the sacred fire
  Might now begin to glow;
Burn up the dross of base desire,
  And make the mountains flow.

O, that it now from heaven might fall,
  And all my sins consume:
Come, Holy Ghost, for thee I call;
  Spirit of burning, come.

Refining fire, go through my heart;
  Illuminate my soul;
Scatter thy life through every part,
  And sanctify the whole.

7.

OH, for a thousand tongues to sing
  My great Redeemer's praise!
The glories of my God and King,
  The triumphs of his grace!

My gracious Master, and my God,
  Assist me to proclaim,
To spread through all the earth abroad,
  The honors of thy name.

He breaks the power of canceled sin,
  He sets the pris'ner free;
His blood can make the foulest clean;
  His blood availed for me.

8.

THERE is a land of pure delight,
  Where saints immortal reign;
Infinite day excludes the night,
  And pleasures banish pain.

There everlasting spring abides,
  And never with'ring flowers:
Death, like a narrow sea, divides
  This heavenly land from ours.

Sweet fields, beyond the swelling flood,
  Stand dressed in living green;
So to the Jews old Canaan stood,
  While Jordan rolled between.

Oh, could we make our doubts remove,
  The gloomy doubts that rise,
And see the Canaan that we love,
  With unbeclouded eyes.

9.

TO Father, Son and Holy Ghost,
  One God whom we adore,
Be glory as it was, is now,
  And shall be evermore.

LISBON. S. M.   DANIEL READ.

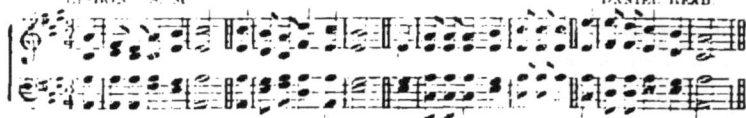

BADEA. S. M.   GERMAN MELODY.

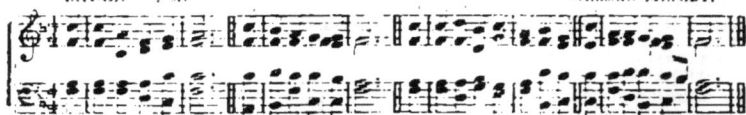

SHIRLAND. S. M.   SAMUEL STANLEY.

STOCKING. S. M.   J. A. MUNK, M. D.

FAIRMOUNT. S. M.   J. H. TENNEY, by per.

ST THOMAS. S. M.   WILLIAMS.

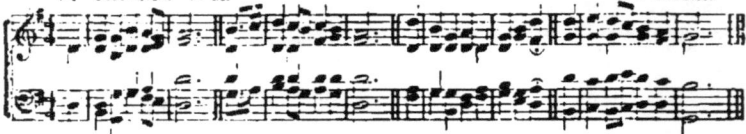

1

RETURN and come to God;
 Cast all your sins away;
Seek ye the Saviour's cleansing blood;
Repent, believe, obey.

Say not ye cannot come;
 For Jesus bled and died,
That none who ask in humble faith,
Should ever be denied.

Say not ye will not come;
 'Tis God vouchsafes to call;
And fearful will their end be found,
On whom his wrath shall fall.

Come then, whoever will,
 Come while 'tis called to-day;
Flee to the Saviour's cleansing blood,
Repent, believe, obey.

2.

OUR sins on Christ were laid;
 He bore the mighty load;
Our ransom-price he fully paid
In groans, and tears, and blood.

To save a world, he dies;
 Sinners, behold the Lamb!
To him lift up your longing eyes;
Seek mercy in his name.

Jesus, we look to thee;—
 Where else can sinners go?
Thy boundless love shall set us free
From wretchedness and woe.

3.

AND can I yet delay
 My little all to give?
To tear my soul from earth away
For Jesus to receive?

Nay, but I yield, I yield;
 I can hold out no more:
I sink, by dying love compell'd,
And own thee conqueror.

Though late, I all forsake;
 My friends, my all, resign;
Gracious Redeemer, take, O take,
And seal me ever thine.

Come, and possess me whole,
 Nor hence again remove;
Settle and fix my wav'ring soul
With all thy weight of love.

4.

DID Christ o'er sinners weep,
 And shall our cheeks be dry?
Let floods of penitential grief
Burst forth from every eye.

The Son of God in tears,
 The wondering angels see!
Be thou astonished, O my soul!
He shed those tears for thee.

He wept that we might weep—
 Each sin demands a tear;
In heaven alone no sin is found,
And there's no weeping there.

5.

BEHOLD the throne of grace!
 The promise calls us near;
There Jesus shows a smiling face,
And waits to answer prayer.

Thine image, Lord, bestow,—
Thy presence and thy love,
That we may serve thee here below,
And reign with thee above.

Teach us to live by faith,
 Conform our wills to thine;
Let us victorious be in death,
And then in glory shine.

6.

A CHARGE to keep I have,
 A God to glorify,
A never-dying soul to save
And fit it for the sky.

To serve the present age,
 My calling to fulfill,
Oh, may it all my powers engage
To do my Master's will.

Arm me with jealous care
 As in thy sight to live,
And, oh, thy servant, Lord, prepare
A strict account to give.

Help me to watch and pray
 And on thyself rely,
Assured, if I my trust betray,
I shall forever die.

7.

OH that I could repent,
 With all my idols part;
And to thy gracious eye present
A humble contrite heart!

Jesus, on me bestow
 The penitent desire;
With true sincerity of woe
My aching breast inspire.

With softening pity look,
 And melt my hardness down;
Strike, with thy love's resistless stroke,
And break this heart of stone!

8.

O COME, and dwell in me,
 Spirit of power within;
And bring the glorious liberty
From sorrow, fear, and sin!

The whole of sin's disease,
 Spirit of health, remove,—
Spirit of perfect holiness,
 Spirit of perfect love.

I want the witness, Lord,
 That all I do is right,—
According to thy will and word,—
 Well-pleasing in thy sight.

I ask no higher state;
 Indulge me but in this,
And soon or later then translate
To my eternal bliss.

9.

COME, ye that love the Lord,
 And let your joys be known,
Join in a song with sweet accord,
While ye surround his throne.

Let those refuse to sing,
 Who never knew our God;
But servants of the heavenly king
May speak their joys abroad.

Then let our songs abound,
 And every tear be dry;
We're marching through Immanuel's ground,
To fairer worlds on high.

92

MARTYN. 7 D.   SIMEON BUTLER MARSH.

PLEYEL'S HYMN 7.   IGNACE PLEYEL.

HORTON. 7.   XAVIER SCHNYDER VON WARTENSEE.

GEBHARDT. 7. D.   ROSSINI.

SEYMOUR. 7.   CARL MARIA VON WEBER.

DURELL. 7s.   By per. of A. N. JOHNSON,   J. OSGOOD.

1.

DEPTH of mercy! can there be
  Mercy still reserved for me?
Can my God his wrath forbear?
Me, the chief of sinners, spare?

I have long withstood his grace,
Long provoked him to his face;
Would not hearken to his calls;
Grieved him by a thousand falls.

Now incline me to repent!
Let me now my fall lament!
Now my foul revolt deplore!
Weep, believe, and sin no more.

2.

WHEN this song of praise shall cease,
  Let thy children, Lord, depart
With the blessing of thy peace,
And thy love in every heart.

Oh, where'er our path may lie,
Father, let us not forget
That we walk beneath thine eye,
That thy care upholds us yet.

Blind are we, and weak and frail;
Be thine aid forever near;
May the fear to sin prevail
Over every other fear.

3.

WE are waiting, blessed Lord,
  In thy courts with one accord;
At thine altars bending low,
Kindred souls together flow;
Yearning love and strong desire
To thy throne of grace aspire,
And with kindling faith we pray—
Holy Spirit, come to-day.

In the closet all alone,
Help us, Christ, to touch the throne!
As we walk, and talk, and sigh,
Hear, oh, hear thy people's cry;
Bring us nearer to thy heart—
We would dwell no more apart;
Sweep the barriers all away—
Holy Spirit, come to-day.

Come to-day—yes, come to-day!
While we wait, and weep, and pray;
Holding fast in Jesus' name
All the promise we may claim,
Come in one grand, glorious hour,
With the burning fire and power
And the wonders, long foretold,
Of the Pentecost of old!

4.

LORD, we come before thee now,
  At thy feet we humbly bow;
Oh! do not our suit disdain;
Shall we seek thee, Lord, in vain?

Lord, on thee our souls depend;
In compassion now descend;
Fill our hearts with thy rich grace,
Tune our lips to sing thy praise.

Send some message to us Lord,
That may joy and peace afford;
Let thy Spirit now impart
Full salvation to each heart.

5.

JESUS! lover of my soul,
  Let me to thy bosom fly,
While the nearer waters roll.
While the tempest still is high;

Hide me, O my Saviour, hide,
  Till the storm of life be past;
Safe into the haven guide—
  O receive my soul at last!

Other refuge have I none;
  Hangs my helpless soul on thee;
Leave, ah! leave me not alone;
  Still support and comfort me.
All my trust on thee is stayed;
  All my help from thee I bring;
Cover my defenceless head
  With the shadow of thy wing.

Plenteous grace with thee is found—
  Grace to cover all my sin;
Let the healing streams abound,
  Make and keep me pure within.
Thou of life the fountain art;
  Freely let me take of thee:
Spring thou up within my heart,
  Rise to all eternity.

6.

CHILDREN of the heavenly King,
  As we journey let us sing;
Sing our Saviour's worthy praise,
Glorious in his works and ways.

We are trav'ling home to God,
In the way our fathers trod;
They are happy now, and we
Soon their happiness shall see.

Fear not, brethren, joyful stand
On the borders of our land;
Jesus Christ, our Father's Son,
Bids us undismayed go on.

Lord! obediently we'll go,
Gladly leaving all below;
Only thou our leader be,
And we still will follow thee!

7.

HASTE, O sinner, to be wise!
  Stay not for the morrow's sun;
Wisdom warns thee, from the skies,
  All the paths of death to shun.

Haste, and mercy now implore;
  Stay not for the morrow's sun;
Thy probation may be o'er
  Ere this evening's work is done.

Haste, while yet thou canst be blest;
  Stay not for the morrow's sun,
Death may thy poor soul arrest,
  Ere the morrow is begun.

8.

COME, my soul, thy suit prepare,
  Jesus loves to answer prayer;
He himself invites thee near,
Bids thee ask him, waits to hear.
Lord, I come to thee for rest;
Take possession of my breast;
There thy blood-bought right maintain,
And without a rival reign.

While I am a pilgrim here
Let thy love my spirit cheer;
As my guide, my guard, my friend,
Lead me to my journey's end.
Show me what I have to do;
Every hour my strength renew;
Let me live a life of faith,
Let me die thy people's death.

94

HAMLINE. 8, 7.

E. A. Hoffman.

TENNEY. C. H. M.

By per. A. N. Johnson.

Refrain.

LENOX. H. M.

Edson.

ALBION. C. M. D.

D. P. Pond.

WILLIE. S.

E. A. Hoffman.

1

SWEET the moments, rich in blessing,
  Which before the cross I spend;
Life and health and peace possessing,
  From the sinner's dying Friend.
Here I sit, in wonder viewing
  Mercy's streams in streams of blood;
Precious drops my soul bedewing,
  Plead and claim my peace with God.

Here it is I find my heaven,
  While upon the Lamb I gaze;
Love I much? I've much forgiven;
  I'm a miracle of grace.
May I still enjoy this feeling,
  In all need to Jesus go;
Prove his death each day more healing,
  And himself more fully know.

2.

O PARADISE! O Paradise!
  Who doth not crave for rest?
Who would not seek the happy land
  Where they that loved are blest?

Ref.—I long to be where Jesus is,
  To be at home in Paradise.

O Paradise! O Paradise!
  I want to sin no more,
I want to be as pure on earth
  As on thy spotless shore.

O Paradise! O Paradise!
  I greatly long to see
The special place my dearest Lord
  In love prepares for me.

3.

ARISE, my soul, arise;
  Shake off thy guilty fears;
The bleeding Sacrifice
  In my behalf appears;
Before the throne my Surety stands,
My name is written on his hands.

The Father hears him pray,
  His dear anointed one:
He cannot turn away
  The presence of his son:
His spirit answers to the blood,
And tells me I am born of God.

My God is reconciled,
  His pard'ning voice I hear:
He owns me for his child,
  I can no longer fear;
With confidence I now draw nigh,
And Father, Abba, Father, cry.

4.

SWEET rivers of redeeming love,
  Lie just below mine eye;
Had I the pinions of a dove,
  I'd to those regions fly;
I'd rise superior to my pain,
  With joy outstrip the wind;
I'd cross bold Jordan's stormy main,
  And leave the world behind.

Oh come, my Saviour, come away,
  And bear me through the sky,
Nor let thy chariot wheels delay,
  Make haste and bring it nigh:
I long to see thy glorious face,
  And in thine image shine;
To triumph in victorious grace,
  And be forever thine.

Then I will tune my harp of gold,
  To my eternal King;
Through ages that can ne'er be told,
  I'll make his praises ring:
All hail I thou great eternal God!
  Who died on Calvary:
And saved me with his precious blood,
  From endless misery.

5.

THOU Shepherd of Israel and mine,
  The joy and desire of my heart,
For closer communion I pine,
  I long to reside where thou art:
Ah! show me that happiest place,
  The place of thy people's abode;
Where saints in an ecstacy gaze,
  And hang on a crucified Lord.

'T is there with the lambs of thy flock,
  There only I covet to rest;
To lie at the foot of the rock,
  Or rise to be hid in thy breast:
'T is there I would always abide,
  And never a moment depart:
Concealed in the cleft of thy side,
  Eternally held in thy heart.

6.

LOVE divine, all love excelling,
  Joy of heaven, to earth come down:
Fix in us thy humble dwelling,
  All thy faithful mercies crown:
Jesus, thou art all compassion;
  Pure, unbounded love thou art;
Visit us with thy salvation,
  Enter every trembling heart.

Breathe, oh breathe thy loving Spirit,
  Into every troubled breast;
Let us all in thee inherit,
  Let us find that second rest;
Come, almighty to deliver,
  Let us all thy life receive:
Suddenly return, and never,
  Never more thy temples leave.

7.

COME, my fond fluttering heart,
  Come, struggle to be free,
Thou and the world must part,
  However hard it be:
My trembling spirit owns it just,
But cleaves yet closer to the dust.

Ye tempting sweets forbear,
  Ye dearest idols fall;
My love ye must not share,
  Jesus shall have it all:
'Tis bitter pain, 'tis cruel smart,
But ah! thou must consent, my heart!

But oh, there is a balm,
  A kind Physician there,
My fevered mind to calm,
  To bid me not despair:
Aid me, dear Saviour, set me free,
And I will all resign to thee.

8.

MAY the grace of Christ our Saviour,
  And the Father's boundless love,
With the Holy Spirit's favor,
  Rest upon us from above.
Thus may we abide in union
  With each other and the Lord,
And possess, in sweet communion,
  Joys which earth cannot afford.

96

ROCK OF AGES. 7, 6 lines.

SIENZA. 6, 5.

EVANGEL. 6, 4.

PEACE. 6, 4.

ROSEFIELD. 7, 6 lines.

1.

MY faith looks up to thee,
Thou Lamb of Calvary;
Saviour divine;
Now hear me while I pray;
Take all my guilt away;
Oh let me, from this day,
Be wholly thine.

May thy rich grace impart,
Strength to my fainting heart;
My zeal inspire;
As thou hast died for me,
Oh may my love to thee,
Pure, warm and changeless be—
A living fire.

While life's dark maze I tread,
And grief around me spread,
Be thou my guide;
Bid darkness turn to day;
Wipe sorrow's tears away,
Nor let me ever stray
From thee aside.

2.

NEARER, my God, to thee,
Nearer to thee:
E'en though it be a cross
That raiseth me;
Still all my song shall be,
Nearer, my God, to thee,
Nearer to thee.

Though like a wanderer,
Daylight all gone,
Darkness be over me,
My rest a stone,
Yet in my dreams I'd be
Nearer, my God, to thee, etc.

There let the way appear
Steps up to heaven;
All that thou sendest me,
In mercy given,
Angels to beckon me
Nearer, my God, to thee, etc.

3.

ROCK of Ages, cleft for me,
Let me hide myself in thee;
Let the water and the blood,
From thy wounded side which flow'd,
Be of sin the double cure,—
Save from wrath and make me pure.

Could my tears forever flow,
Could my zeal no languor know,
These for sin could not atone;
Thou must save, and thou alone:
In my hand no price I bring;
Simply to the cross I cling.

While I draw this fleeting breath,
When my eyes shall close in death,
When I rise to worlds unknown,
And behold thee on thy throne,
Rock of Ages, cleft for me,
Let me hide myself in thee.

4.

BLESSED Jesus, thou art mine,
All I have is wholly thine;
Thou dost dwell within my heart,
Thou dost reign in every part:
Blessed Jesus, keep me white,
Keep me walking in the light.

I am safe within the fold,
All my cares on thee are rolled,
I enjoy the sweetest rest,
For I'm leaning on thy breast;
Blessed Jesus, keep me white,
Keep me walking in the light.

Precious Jesus, day by day,
Keep me in the holy way;
Keep my mind in perfect peace;
Every day my faith increase:
Blessed Jesus, keep me white,
Keep me walking in the light.

5.

TAKE my life and let it be
Consecrated, Lord to thee.
Take my hands and let them move
At the impulse of thy love.

REFRAIN.

Take myself and let me be
Ever only all for thee.

Take my moments and my days,
Let them flow in ceaseless praise.
Take my will and make it thine,
Let it be no longer mine.

Take my heart, it is thine own,
Let it be thy royal throne.
Take my love, my Lord of power,
At thy feet its treasures store.

6.

WHEN shall we meet again,
Meet ne'er to sever?
When will peace wreathe her chain
Round us forever?
Our hearts will ne'er repose,
Safe from each blast that blows,
In this dark vale of woes,
Never—no, never!

When shall love freely flow
Pure as life's river?
When shall sweet friendship glow
Changeless forever?
Where joys celestial thrill,
Where bliss each heart shall fill,
And fears of parting chill
Never—no, never!

Up to that world of light
Take us, dear Saviour;
May we all there unite,
Happy forever;
Where kindred spirits dwell,
There may our music swell,
And time our joys dispel
Never—no, never!

7.

COME, Holy Ghost, in love,
Shed on us from above
Thine own bright ray!
Divinely good thou art;
Thy sacred gifts impart
To gladden each sad heart:
O come to-day!

Come, tenderest Friend, and best,
Our most delightful Guest,
With soothing power:
Rest, which the weary know,
Shade, 'mid the noontide glow,
Peace, when deep griefs o'erflow,
Cheer us this hour!

Come, Light serene, and still,
Our inmost bosoms fill,
Dwell in each breast;
We know no dawn but thine,
Send forth thy beams divine,
On our dark souls to shine,
And make us blest!

98

BARTIMEUS. 8 & 7.

SICILIAN HYMN. 8 & 7.

WEBB. 7 & 6.

NETTLETON. 8, 7, 4.

MAYTOWN. 8, 7, 4.   By per. of A. N. Johnson.   John Mason.

1.

COME, ye sinners, poor and needy,
  Weak and wounded, sick and sore,
Jesus ready stands to save you,
  Full of pity, love and power:
    He is able,
He is willing, doubt no more.

Now ye needy, come and welcome,
God's free bounty glorify;
True belief and true repentance,
  Every grace that brings you nigh,
    Without money,
Come to Jesus Christ and buy.

Come, ye weary, heavy-laden,
  Bruised and mangled by the fall,
If you tarry till you're better,
  You will never come at all;
    Not the righteous,
Sinners, Jesus came to call.

2.

OH, thou God of my salvation,
  My Redeemer from all sin;
Moved by thy divine compassion,
  Who hast died my heart to win;
    I will praise thee:
Where shall I thy praise begin?

Though unseen, I love the Saviour;
  He hath brought salvation near;
Manifests his pard'ning favor;
  And when Jesus doth appear,
    Soul and body
Shall his glorious image bear.

Angels now are hov'ring round us,
  Unperceived amid the throng;
Wond'ring at the love that crowned us,
  Glad to join the holy song;
    Hallelujah,
Love and praise to Christ belong!

3.

COME thou fount of every blessing,
  Tune my heart to sing thy grace;
Streams of mercy, never ceasing,
  Call for songs of loudest praise,
Teach me some melodious sonnet,
  Sung by flaming tongues above;
Praise the mount—I'm fixed upon it,
  Mount of thy redeeming love.

Here I'll raise mine Ebenezer;
  Hither by thy help I'm come;
And I hope by thy good pleasure,
  Safely to arrive at home.
Jesus sought me when a stranger,
  Wand'ring from the fold of God;
He, to rescue me from danger,
  Interposed his precious blood.

Oh, to grace how great a debtor
  Daily I'm constrained to be!
Let thy goodness like a fetter,
  Bind my wand'ring heart to thee.
Prone to wander, Lord, I feel it—
  Prone to leave the God I love;
Here's my heart, oh take and seal it—
  Seal it for thy courts above.

4.

LORD, dismiss us with thy blessing;
  Fill our hearts with joy and peace;
Let us each, thy love possessing,
  Triumph in redeeming grace;
    Oh refresh us,
Traveling through this wilderness.

Thanks we give, and adoration,
  For thy gospel's joyful sound;
May the fruits of thy salvation
  In our hearts and lives abound;
    May thy presence
With us evermore be found.

So, when'er the signal's given,
  Us from earth to call away,
Borne on angels' wings to heaven,
  Glad the summons to obey,
    May we ever
Reign with Christ in endless day.

5.

NOW the solemn shadows darken,
  And the daylight slowly dies,
Holy Saviour, thou wilt hearken
  When thy children's prayers arise,
    Blessed Jesus!
Look on us with loving eyes.

Some are tried with doubts and dangers,
  Some have found their hearts grow cold,
Some are aliens now, and strangers
  To the faith they loved of old;
    Blessed Jesus!
Bring them back into thy fold.

Some in conflict sore have striven
  With temptation fierce and strong;
Lord, to them let strength be given
  If the battle should be long!
    Blessed Jesus!
Change our mourning into song.

6.

IN the cross of Christ I glory,
  Towering o'er the wrecks of time;
All the light of sacred story
  Gathers round its head sublime.

When the woes of life o'ertake me,
  Hopes deceive, and fears annoy,
Never shall the cross forsake me;
  Lo! it glows with peace and joy.

Bane and blessing, pain and pleasure,
  By the cross are sanctified:
Peace is there, that knows no measure,
  Joys, that through all time abide.

7.

STAND up!—stand up for Jesus!
  Ye soldiers of the cross;
Lift high his royal banner,
  It must not suffer loss;
From victory unto victory
  His army shall be led,
Till every foe is vanquished,
  And Christ is Lord indeed.

Stand up!—stand up for Jesus!
  Stand in his strength alone:
The arm of flesh will fail you—
  Ye dare not trust your own:
Put on the gospel armor,
  And, watching unto prayer,
Where duty calls or danger,
  Be never wanting there.

Stand up!—stand up for Jesus!
  The strife will not be long;
This day the noise of battle,
  The next the victor's song:
To him that overcometh,
  A crown of life shall be:
He, with the King of glory,
  Shall reign eternally.

1.

I HAVE entered the valley of blessing
so sweet,
And Jesus abides with me there;
And his Spirit and blood make my cleans-
ing complete,
And his perfect love casteth out fear.

Cho.—O come to this valley of blessing so sweet,
Where Jesus will fullness bestow,
And believe, and receive, and confess him,
That all his salvation may know.

There is love in the valley of blessing so
sweet,
Such as none but the blood-washed may
feel;
When heaven comes down redeemed spirits
to greet,
And Christ sets his covenant seal.

There's a song in the valley of blessing so
sweet,
That angels would fain join the strain;
As with rapturous praises we bow at his feet,
Crying, Worthy the Lamb that was slain.

2.

I HAVE a Saviour, he's pleading in glory,
A dear, loving Saviour though earth-
friends be few;
And now he is watching in tenderness o'er
me,
And oh that my Saviour were your
Saviour too!

Cho.—For you I am praying,
For you I am praying,
For you I am praying,
I'm praying for you.

I have a Father: to me he has given
A hope for eternity, blessed and true;
And soon will he call me to meet him in
heaven,
But oh that he'd let me bring you with
me too!

I have a peace: it is calm as a river—
A peace that the friends of this world
never knew;
My Saviour alone is its Author and Giver,
And oh, could I know it was given to you!

3.

THERE'S a wideness in God's mercy,
Like the wideness of the sea;
There's a kindness in his justice,
Which is more than liberty.

Cho.—He is calling, "Come to me;"
Lord, I'll gladly haste to thee.

There is welcome for the sinner
And more graces for the good;
There is mercy for the Saviour;
There is healing in his blood.

If our love were but more simple,
We should take him at his word;
And our lives would be all sunshine
In the sweetness of our Lord.

4.

O BLISS of the purified! bliss of the free!
I plunge in the crimson tide open'd
for me!
O'er sin and uncleanness exulting I stand,
And point to the print of the nails in his
hand.

Cho.—O! sing of his mighty love—mighty
to save.

O bliss of the purified, Jesus is mine,
No longer in dread condemnation I pine;
In conscious salvation I sing of his grace
Who lifted upon me the smiles of his face!

O bliss of the purified! bliss of the pure;
No wound hath the soul that his blood
cannot cure;
No sorrow-bowed head but may sweetly
find rest,
No tears—but may dry them on Jesus's
breast.

5.

I KNOW not if the dark or bright
Shall be my lot,
If that wherein my soul delight
Be best or not;
It may be mine to drag for years
Toil's heavy chain,
Or day and night my meat be tears,
On bed of pain.

Chorus.

But this I know, there is a hand divine
That holds me still, whatever lot be mine,
But this I know, where'er I go, there is a
hand divine,
That holds me still, thro' every ill, what-
ever lot be mine.

My bark is wafted to the strand
By breath divine,
And on the helm there rests a hand
More strong than mine:
One who has known in storms to sail
I have on board;
Above the raging of the gale,
I hear my Lord.

He holds me 'midst the billows' might,
I shall not fall;
If sharp, 'tis short; if long, 'tis light;
He tempers all—
Safe to the land, safe to the land,
The end is this:
And then with him go hand in hand,
Far into bliss.

6.

SAVIOUR, like a shepherd lead us;
Much we need thy tend'rest care;
In thy pleasant pastures feed us,
For our use thy folds prepare.
Blessed Jesus, thou hast bought us, thine we are.

We are thine, do thou befriend us;
Be the guardian of our way;
Keep thy flock, from sin defend us,
Seek us when we go astray.
Blessed Jesus, hear, O hear us when we pray.

Thou hast promised to receive us,
Poor and sinful though we be;
Thou hast mercy to relieve us,
Grace to cleanse, and power to free.
Blessed Jesus, we will early turn to thee.

7.

PRAISE the name of God most high,
Praise him, all below the sky,
Praise him, all ye heavenly host,
Father, Son and Holy Ghost;
As through countless ages past,
Evermore his praise shall last.

1.

IN some way or other the Lord will provide:
It may not be *my* way,
It may not be *thy* way;
And yet, in his *own* way,
"The Lord will provide."

Cho.— Then we'll trust in the Lord,
And he will provide;
Yes, we'll trust in the Lord,
And he will provide.

At some time or other the Lord will provide:
It may not be *my* time,
It may not be *thy* time;
And yet in his *own* time,
"The Lord will provide."

Depend then no longer: the Lord will provide;
And this be the token—
No word he hath spoken
Was ever yet broken:
"The Lord will provide."

2.

PRECIOUS promise God hath given
To the weary passer by,
On the way from earth to heaven,
"I will guide thee with mine eye."

Cho.—I will guide thee, I will guide thee,
I will guide thee with mine eye;
On the way from earth to heaven,
I will guide thee with mine eye.

When temptations almost win thee,
And thy trusted watchers fly,
Let this promise ring within thee,
"I will guide thee with mine eye."

When thy secret hopes have perished,
In the grave of years gone by,
Let this promise still be cherished,
"I will guide thee with mine eye."

3.

WE speak of the realms of the blessed,
That country so bright and so fair;
And oft are its glories confessed,
But what must it be to be there.

Cho.—Over there, over there,
O, what must it be to be there.

We speak of its freedom from sin,
From sorrow, temptation and care,
From trials without and within—
But what must it be to be there!

Do thou, Lord, mid'st pleasure or woe
For heaven my spirit prepare;
And shortly I also shall know,
And feel what it is to be there.

4.

I LEFT it all with Jesus Long ago;
All my sins I brought him, And my woe,
When by faith I saw him On the tree,
Heard his small, still whisper, 'Tis for thee;'
From my heart the burden Rolled away—
Happy day.
I leave it all with Jesus Day by day;
Faith can firmly trust him Come what may.
Hope has dropped her anchor, Found her rest
In the calm, sure haven Of his breast;
Love esteems it heaven To abide
At his side.

O, leave it all with Jesus, Drooping soul!
Tell not half the story, But the whole;
Worlds on worlds are hanging On his hand,
Life and death are waiting His command;
Yet his tender bosom Makes thee room—
O come home!

5.

I LOVE to tell the story
Of unseen things above,
Of Jesus and his glory,
Of Jesus and his love;
I love to tell the story,
Because I know it's true,
It satisfies my longings,
As nothing else would do.

Cho.—I love to tell the story,
'Twill be my theme in glory
To tell the old, old story,
Of Jesus and his love.

I love to tell the story;
More wonderful it seems
Than all the golden fancies
Of all our golden dreams.
I love to tell the story;
It did so much for me!
And that is just the reason
I tell it now to thee.

6.

I LAY my sins on Jesus, The spotless Lamb
of God;
He bears them all and frees us From the
accursed load.

Cho.—Hallelujah, Jesus saves me, He makes
me "white as snow."

I bring my guilt to Jesus, To wash my
crimson stains
White, in his blood most precious, Till not
a spot remains.

I lay my wants on Jesus— All fullness dwells
in him;
He healeth my diseases, He doth my soul
redeem.

7.

THERE'S a highway for the ransomed,
where the children of the King,
Upon their pilgrim journey triumphantly
may sing,
Of a Saviour who redeemed them, and de-
livers from all sin.
His blood NOW makes me clean.

Cho.—Glory, glory, hallelujah!
Glory, glory, hallelujah!
Glory, glory, hallelujah!
His blood NOW keeps me clean.

I was pardoned by God's mercy, but at heart
was evil still,
A carnal mind was in me, which resolves
could never kill.
But, blessed be his holy name, he changes
heart and will!
His blood NOW makes me clean.

Now, like pebbles in the running brook that
'neath the ripples lay,
My heart is sweetly kept from sin each
moment, night and day;
And as faith the conquest gave me, I bid
doubts to go their way,
His blood NOW makes me clean!

On the mountain tops of Beulah or in the
vale below,
Where temptations' wildest hurricanes their
fiercest tempests blow,
In sorrow or in conflict his grace he doth
bestow,
His blood NOW makes me clean!

1.

TELL me the old, old story,
　Of unseen things above;
Of Jesus and his glory,
　Of Jesus and his love.
Tell me the story simply,
　As to a little child;
For I am weak and weary,
　And helpless and defiled.

Cho.—Tell me the old, old story,
　　Of Jesus and his love.

Tell me the story slowly,
　That I may take it in;
That wonderful redemption,
　God's remedy for sin.
Tell me the story often,
　For I forget so soon,
The "early dew" of morning
　Has passed away at noon.

Tell me the story softly,
　With earnest tones, and grave;
Remember, I'm the sinner
　Whom Jesus came to save;
Tell me the story always,
　If you would really be
In any time of trouble
　A comforter to me.

2.

IN the Christian's home in glory,
　There remains a land of rest.
Where the Saviour's gone before me
　To fulfil my soul's request.

Cho.—On the other side of Jordan,
　　In the sweet fields of Eden,
　　Where the tree of life is blooming,
　　There is rest for you.
　　There is rest for the weary,
　　There is rest for you.

Pain or sickness ne'er can enter;
　Grief nor woe my lot shall share;
But in that celestial center
　I, a crown of life shall wear.

Sing, O sing, ye heirs of glory,
　Shout your triumph as you go;
Zion's gates will open to you,
　You shall find an entrance through.

3.

HE leadeth me! oh! blessed thought;
　Oh! words which heav'nly comfort fraught;
Whate'er I do, where'er I be,
Still 'tis God's hand that leadeth me.

Ref.—He leadeth me, He leadeth me!
　　By his own hand he leadeth me;
　　His faithful follower I would be,
　　For by his hand he leadeth me.

Sometimes 'mid scenes of deepest gloom,
Sometimes where Eden's bowers bloom,
By waters still, o'er troubled sea,
Still 'tis his hand that leadeth me.

Lord, I would clasp thy hand in mine,
Nor ever murmur nor repine—
Content, whatever lot I see,
Since 'tis my God that leadeth me.

4.

ALL glory to the bleeding lamb,
　Who died on Calvary!
Yes, glory to the bleeding Lamb
Who saves and ransoms me!

Cho.—I've been redeem'd, I've been redeem'd,
Been wash'd in the blood of the Lamb.
Been redeem'd by the blood of the Lamb,
That flow'd on Calvary.

The blood that my Redeemer spilt,
　The blood, so rich and free,
That cleanses sinful heart from guilt,
　Now saves and cleanses me.

I am redeemed—O blessed state!
　I am redeemed from sin,
O, love so infinitely great!
　The blood has made me clean.

5.

THERE were ninety and nine that safely
　lay
　In the shelter of the fold.
But one was out on the hills away,
　Far off from the gates of gold—
Away on the mountains wild and bare,
Away from the tender Shepherd's care.

"Lord, thou hast here thy ninety and nine:
　Are they not enough for thee?"
But the Shepherd made answer: "This of
　mine
　Has wandered away from me:
And although the road be rough and steep,
I go to the desert to find my sheep.

But none of the ransomed ever knew
　How deep were the waters crossed;
Nor how dark was the night that the Lord
　passed through
Ere he found his sheep that was lost.
Out in the desert he heard its cry—
Sick and helpless, and ready to die.

But all through the mountains, thunder-
　riven,
　And up from the rocky steep,
There rose a cry to the gate of heaven,
　"Rejoice! I have found my sheep!"
And the angels echoed around the throne,
"Rejoice, for the Lord brings back his own!"

6.

SOWING the seed by the day-light fair,
　Sowing the seed by the noon-day glare,
Sowing the seed by the fading light,
Sowing the seed in the solemn night,
‖: Oh, what shall the harvest be? :‖

Cho.—Sown in the darkness or sown in the
　　light,
　　Sown in our weakness or sown in our
　　might,
　　Gathered in time or eternity,
　　Sure, ah, sure will the harvest, harvest
　　be.

Sowing the seed by the way-side high,
Sowing the seed on the rock to die,
Sowing the seed where the thorns will spoil,
Sowing the seed in the fertile soil.
‖: Oh, what shall the harvest be? :‖

Sowing the seed with an aching heart,
Sowing the seed while the teardrops start,
Sowing in hope till the reapers come
Gladly to gather the harvest home,
‖: Oh, what shall the harvest be? :‖

1.

I GAVE my life for thee
My precious blood I shed,
That thou might'st ransomed be,
And quickened from the dead;
I gave, I gave my life for thee,
What hast thou given for me?

My Father's house of light,—
My glory-circled throne,
I left, for earthly night,
For wand'rings sad and lone;
I left. I left it all for thee;
Hast thou left aught for me?

And I have brought to thee,
Down from my home above,
Salvation full and free,
My pardon and my love;
I bring, I bring rich gifts to thee,
What hast thou brought to me.

2.

WHAT a friend we have in Jesus,
All our sins and griefs to bear;
What a privilege to carry
Everything to God in prayer,
O, what peace we often forfeit,
O, what needless pain we bear—
All because we do not carry
Everything to God in prayer.

Have we trials and temptations?
Is there trouble anywhere?
We should never be discouraged,
Take it to the Lord in prayer.
Can we find a Friend so faithful,
Who will all our sorrows share?
Jesus knows our every weakness,
Take it to the Lord in prayer.

Are we weak and heavy laden,
Cumbered with a load of care?
Precious Saviour, still our refuge,
Take it to the Lord in prayer.
Do thy friends despise, forsake thee?
Take it to the Lord in prayer;
In his arms he'll take and shield thee,
Thou wilt find a solace there.

3.

LORD, I hear of showers of blessing
Thou art scatt'ring full and free;
Showers, the thirsty land refreshing:
Let some droppings fall on me—Even me.

Love of God—so pure and changeless;
Blood of Christ—so rich and free:
Grace of God—so strong and boundless;
Magnify it all in me—Even me.

Pass me not—thy lost one bringing;
Bend my heart, O Lord, to thee;
Whilst the streams of life are springing,
Blessing others, O, bless me—Even me.

4.

THERE is life for a look at the crucified
One,
There is life at this moment for thee:
Then look. sinner, look unto him and be
saved,
Unto him who was nailed to the tree.

Ref.—Look! look! look and live!
There is life for a look at the crucified One,
There is life at this moment for
thee.

It is not thy tears of repentance and prayers,
But the blood that atones for the soul;
On him, then, who shed it, thou mayest at
once
Thy weight of iniquities roll.

Then take with rejoicing from Jesus at once
The life everlasting he gives;
And know with assurance thou never canst
die
Since Jesus, thy righteousness, lives.

5.

WE praise thee, O God! for the Son of thy
love,
For Jesus, who died, and is now gone above.

Cho.—Hallelujah! Thine the glory, Hallelujah! amen. etc.

We praise thee, O God! for thy Spirit of light,
Who has shown us our Saviour, and scattered our night.

All glory and praise, to the Lamb that was
slain,
Who has borne all our sins and has cleansed
every stain.

All glory and praise to the God of all grace,
Who has bought us, and sought us, and
guided our ways.

6.

COME, my Redeemer, come,
And deign to dwell with me;
Come, and thy right assume,
And bid thy rivals flee:
Come, my Redeemer, quickly come,
And make my heart thy lasting home.

Cho.—Whiter than snow, whiter than snow,
Wash me in the blood of the Lamb,
And I shall be whiter than snow.

Exert thy mighty power,
And banish all my sin;
In this auspicious hour,
Bring all thy graces in:
Come, my Redeemer, quickly come,
And make my heart thy lasting home.

Rule thou in every thought
And passion of my soul,
Till all my powers are brought
Beneath thy full control:
Come, my Redeemer, quickly come,
And make my heart thy lasting home.

7.

TO-DAY the Saviour calls;
Ye wand'rers come!
O, ye benighted souls,
Why longer roam?

To-day the Saviour calls!
For refuge fly;
The storm of vengence falls,
Ruin is nigh.

To-day the Saviour calls!
Oh, listen now!
Within these sacred walls
To Jesus bow.

The Spirit calls to-day:
Yield to his power;
Oh, grieve him not away!
'Tis mercy's hour.

1.

SWEET hour of prayer! sweet hour of
prayer!
That calls me from a world of care,
And bids me at my Father's throne,
Make all my wants and wishes known.
In seasons of distress and grief,
My soul has often found relief;
And oft escaped the tempter's snare,
By thy return, sweet hour of prayer.

Sweet hour of prayer! sweet hour of prayer!
Thy wings shall my petitions bear
To him whose truth and faithfulness
Engage the waiting soul to bless:
And since he bids me seek his face,
Believe his word, and trust his grace,
I'll cast on him my every care,
And wait for thee, sweet hour of prayer.

2.

BEHOLD a stranger at the door!
He gently knocks, has knocked before,
Has waited long, is waiting still;
You treat no other friend so ill.

Cho.—Oh, let the dear Saviour come in,
He'll cleanse thy heart from sin!
Oh, keep him no more out at the door,
But let the dear Saviour come in.

Oh, lovely attitude!—he stands
With melting heart, and loaded hands,
Oh, matchless kindness!—and he shows
This matchless kindness to his foes!

But will he prove a friend indeed?
He will—the very friend you need;
The friend of sinners—yes, 'tis he,
With garments dyed on Calvary.

Rise, touched with gratitude divine,
Turn out his enemy and thine,—
That soul destroying monster, sin,—
And let the heavenly Stranger in.

3.

I AM thine own, O Christ—
Henceforth entirely thine;
And life from this glad hour,
New life is mine!

Cho.—O, peace! O, holy rest,
O, balmy breath of love!
O, heart divinest, best,
Thy depth I prove.

No earthly joy shall lure
My quiet soul from thee:
This deep delight, so pure,
Is heav'n to me.

I cannot tell the art
By which such bliss is given:
I know thou hast my heart,
And I—have heaven!

4.

MY hope is built on nothing less
Than Jesus' blood and righteousness;
I dare not trust the sweetest frame,
But wholly lean on Jesus' name.

On Christ, the solid Rock, I stand;
All other ground is sinking sand.

When darkness seems to vail his face,
I rest on his unchanging grace;
In every high and stormy gale
My anchor holds within the vail.

His oath, his covenant, and blood,
Support me in the 'whelming flood:
When all around my soul gives way,
He then is all my hope and stay.

5.

O, TO be nothing, nothing,
Only to lie at his feet,
A broken and emptied vessel,
For the Master's use made meet.
Emptied that he might fill me
As forth to his service I go;
Broken, that so unhindered,
His life through me might flow.

O, to be nothing, nothing,
Only as led by his hand;
A messenger at his gateway,
Only waiting for his command;
Only an instrument ready
His praises to sound at his will,
Willing, should he not require me
In silence to wait on him still.

O, to be nothing, nothing,
Painful the humbling may be:
Yet low in the dust I'd lay me
That the world might my Saviour see.
Rather be nothing, nothing,—
To him let their voices be raised;
He is the Fountain of blessing,
He only is most to be praised.

6.

I STAND all bewildered with wonder,
And gaze on the ocean of love;
And over its waves to my spirit
Come peace, like a heavenly dove.

Cho.—The cross now covers my sins,
The past is under the blood;
I'm trusting in Jesus for all,
My will is the will of my God.

I struggled and wrestled to win it,
The blessing that setteth me free;
But, when I had ceased from my struggles,
His peace Jesus gave unto me.

He laid his hand on me and heal'd me,
And bade me be every whit whole;
I touched but the hem of his garment,
And glory came thrilling my soul.

7.

O JESUS, delight of my soul,
My Saviour, my Shepherd divine,
I yield to thy blessed control;
My body and spirit are thine:
Thy love I can never deserve,
That bids me be happy in thee:
My God and my King I will serve,
Whose favor is heaven to me.

How can I thy goodness repay,
By nature so weak and defiled?
Myself I have given away;
Oh, call me thine own blessed child;
And art thou my Father above?
Will Jesus abide in my heart?
Oh, bind me so fast with thy love,
That I from thee ne'er shall depart.

8.

TO thee be praise forever,
Thou glorious King of kings:
Thy wondrous love and favor
Each ransomed spirit sings;
We'll celebrate thy glory
With all thy saints above,
And shout the joyful story
Of thy redeeming love.

1.

YET there is room! the Lamb's bright hall
    of song,
With its fair glory, beckons thee along;
Room, room, still room! Oh, enter, enter
    now!

Yet there is room! Still open stands the gate,
The gate of love; it is not yet too late;
Room, room, still room! oh, enter, enter
    now!

Pass in, pass in! that banquet is for thee;
That cup of everlasting love is free;
Room, room, still room! oh, enter, enter
    now.

Ere night that gate may close and seal thy
    doom;
Then the last, low, long cry, "No room, no
    room!"
No room, no room; oh, woeful cry, "No
    room!"

2.

JESUS saves me every day,
    Jesus saves me every night;
Jesus saves me all the way,
    Thro' the darkness, thro' the light.

Cho.—Jesus saves, O bliss sublime,
    Jesus saves me all the time.

Jesus saves me, he is mine;
    Jesus saves me, I am his;
Jesus saves while I recline
    On his precious promises.

Jesus saves, he saves from sin;
    Jesus saves, I feel him nigh;
Jesus saves, he dwells within;
    Gladly do I testify.

3.

PRECIOUS Saviour thou dost save me;
    Thine, and only thine I am.
O! the cleansing blood has reached me;
    Glory, glory to the Lamb.

Glory, glory, Jesus saves me; Glory, glory
    to the Lamb!
Oh! the cleansing blood has reached me;
    Glory, glory to the Lamb!

Long my yearning heart was trying
    To enjoy this perfect rest;
But I gave all trying over;
    Simply trusting, I was blest.

Consecrated to thy service,
    I will live and die for thee;
I will witness to thy glory,
    Of salvation full and free.

4.

YIELD not to temptation,
    For yielding is sin,
Each victory will help you
    Some other to win;
Fight manfully onward,
    Dark passions subdue,
Look ever to Jesus,
    He'll carry you through.

Cho.—Ask the Saviour to help you,
    Comfort, strengthen and keep you;
He is willing to aid you,
    He'll carry you through.

Shun evil companions,
    Bad language disdain,
God's name hold in rev'rence,
    Nor take it in vain;
Be thoughtful and earnest,
    Kind-hearted and true,
Look ever to Jesus,
    He'll carry you through.

To him that o'er cometh,
    God giveth a crown,
Thro' faith we shall conquer,
    Though often cast down;
He, who is our Saviour,
    Our strength will renew,
Look ever to Jesus,
    He'll carry you through.

5.

THERE is a spot to me more dear
    Than native vale or mountain;
A spot for which affection's tear
    Springs grateful from its fountain:
'Tis not where kindred souls abound,
    Though that is almost heaven;
But where I first my Saviour found,
    And felt my sins forgiven.

Sinking and panting as for breath,
    I knew not help was near me;
And cried "Oh! save me, Lord, from death,
    Immortal Jesus, hear me."
Then quick as thought I felt him mine,
    My Saviour stood before me;
I saw his brightness round me shine,
    And shouted, "Glory! Glory!"

O sacred hour! O hallowed spot!
    Where love divine first found me;
Wherever falls my distant lot,
    My heart shall linger round thee;
And when from earth I rise to soar
    Up to my home in heaven,
Down will I cast my eyes once more,
    Where I was first forgiven.

6.

I'M but a stranger here—
    Heaven is my home;
Earth is a desert drear—
    Heaven is my home;
Danger and sorrow stand
    Round me on every hand—
Heaven is my fatherland;
    Heaven is my home.

What though the tempests rage?
    Heaven is my home;
Short is my pilgrimage—
    Heaven is my home;
And time's wild, wintry blast
    Soon will be overpast;
I shall reach home at last—
    Heaven is my home.

7.

MY heavenly home is bright and fair;
    Nor pain, nor death can enter there;
Its glittering towers the sun outshine;
    That heavenly mansion shall be mine.

Cho.—We're going home, to die no more.

My Father's house is built on high,
    Far, far above the starry sky:
When from this earthly prison free,
    That heavenly mansion mine shall be.

Let others seek a home below
    Which flames devour, or waves o'erflow;
Be mine the happier lot to own
    A heavenly mansion near the throne.

1

JESUS, let thy pitying eye
 Call back a wand'ring sheep:
False to thee, like Peter, I
 Would fain like Peter weep.
Let me be by grace restored:
 On me be all long-suff'ring shown;
Turn, and look upon me, Lord,
 And break my heart of stone.

Saviour, Prince, enthroned above,
 Repentance to impart,
Give me through thy dying love,
 The humble, contrite heart:
Give me, what I have long implored,
 True penitence for sins unknown:
Turn, and look upon me, Lord,
 And break my heart of stone.

For thine own compassion's sake,
 The gracious wonder show;
Cast my sins behind thy back,
 And wash me white as snow;
Speak the reconciling word,
 And let thy mercy melt me down;
Turn, and look upon me, Lord,
 And break my heart of stone.

2.

BY thy birth, and by thy tears;
 By thy human griefs and fears;
By thy conflict in the hour
Of the subtle tempter's power—
Saviour, look with pitying eye;
Saviour, help me, or I die.

By thy lonely hour of prayer;
By the fearful conflict there;
By thy cross and dying cries;
By thy one great sacrifice,—
Saviour, look with pitying eye;
Saviour, help me, or I die.

By thy triumph o'er the grave;
By thy power the lost to save;
By thy high, majestic throne;
By the empire all thine own,—
Saviour, look with pitying eye;
Saviour, help me, or I die.

3.

HOW tedious and tasteless the hours,
 When Jesus no longer I see;
Sweet prospects, sweet birds, and sweet flowers
Have all lost their sweetness to me:
The midsummer sun shines but dim,
 The fields strive in vain to look gay;
But when I am happy in him,
 December's as pleasant as May.

His name yields the richest perfume,
 And sweeter than music his voice;
His presence disperses my gloom,
 And makes all within me rejoice;
I should, were he always thus nigh,
 Have nothing to wish or to fear,
No mortal so happy as I,
 My summer would last all the year.

4.

DEAR Jesus, I long to be perfectly whole;
 I want thee forever to live in my soul;
Break down every idol, cast out every foe;
Now wash me, and I shall be whiter than
 snow.

Whiter than snow, yes, whiter than snow,
Now wash me, and I shall be whiter than snow.

Dear Jesus, let nothing unholy remain;
Apply thine own blood and extract every
 stain;
To have this blest cleansing, I all things
 forego;
Now wash me and I shall be whiter than
 snow.

The blessing by faith I receive from above,
O, glory! my soul is made perfect in love;
My prayer has prevailed, and this moment
 I know
The blood is applied—I am whiter than snow.

5.

MY body, soul, and spirit, Jesus, I give to
 thee,
 A consecrated off'ring, thine evermore
 to be.

Cho.—My all is on the altar, I'm waiting for
 the fire;
 Waiting, waiting, waiting, I'm waiting for the fire.

O! let the fire descending Just now upon
 my soul,
Consume my humble offering, And cleanse
 and make me whole.

I'm thine, O blessed Jesus, Washed by thy
 precious blood,
Now seal me by thy Spirit, A sacrifice to
 God.

6.

WHAT means this eager, anxious throng,
 Which moves with busy haste along—
These wondrous gatherings day by day?
What means this strange commotion, pray?
In accents hush'd the throng reply;
"Jesus of Nazareth passeth by."

Ho! all ye heavy laden come:
Here's pardon, comfort, rest, and home,
Ye wanderers from a Father's face,
Return, accept his proffered grace,
Ye tempted ones, there's refuge nigh,
"Jesus of Nazareth passeth by."

But if you still this call refuse,
And all his wondrous love abuse,
Soon will he sadly from you turn,
Your bitter prayer for pardon spurn,
"Too late! too late!" will be the cry—
"Jesus of Nazareth has passed by."

7.

THERE is a fountain filled with blood,
 Drawn from Immanuel's veins,
And sinners plunged beneath that flood
 Lose all their guilty stains.

The dying thief rejoiced to see
 That fountain in his day;
And there may I, though vile as he,
 Wash all my sins away.

Thou dying Lamb! thy precious blood
 Shall never lose its power,
Till all the ransomed Church of God
 Are saved to sin no more.

E'er since by faith I saw the stream
 Thy flowing wounds supply,
Redeeming love has been my theme,
 And shall be till I die.

Then in a nobler, sweeter song
 I'll sing Thy power to save,
When this poor, lisping, stammering tongue
 Lies silent in the grave.

1.

THE mistakes of my life have been many,
  The sins of my heart have been more,
And I scarce can see for weeping,
But I'll knock at the open door.

Cho.—I know I am weak and sinful,
  It comes to me more and more;
But when the dear Saviour shall bid
  me come in,
  I'll enter the open door.

I am lowest of those who love him,
  I am weakest of those who pray;
But I come as he has bidden,
  And he will not say me nay.

My mistakes his free grace will cover,
  My sins he will wash away,
And the feet that shrink and falter
  Shall walk thro' the gates of day.

The mistakes of my life have been many,
  And my spirit is sick with sin,
And I scarce can see for weeping,
  But the Saviour will let me in.

2.

JESUS, I my cross have taken,
  All to leave and follow thee:
Naked, poor, despised, forsaken,
  Thou from hence my all shalt be.
Perish every fond ambition,
  All I've sought, or hoped, or known;
Yet how rich is my condition!
  God and heaven are still my own.

Let the world despise and leave me,
  They have left my Saviour too;
Human hearts and looks deceive me:—
  Thou art not, like them, untrue.
And while thou shalt smile upon me,
  God of wisdom, love, and might,
Foes may hate and friends may shun me,
  Show thy face and all is bright.

3.

O, NOW I see the crimson wave,
  The fountain deep and wide;
Jesus, my Lord, mighty to save,
  Points to his wounded side.

Cho.—The cleansing stream, I see, I see!
  I plunge, and O, it cleanseth me;
O, praise the Lord, it cleanseth me!
  It cleanseth me, yes, cleanseth me!

I see the new creation rise,
  I hear the speaking blood;
It speaks! polluted nature dies!
  Sinks 'neath the cleansing flood.

I rise to walk in heaven's own light,
  Above the world and sin,
With heart made pure, and garments white,
  And Christ enthroned within.

4.

I WILL sing you a song of that beautiful
  land,
  The far away home of the soul,
Where no storms ever beat on the glittering
  strand,
  While the years of eternity roll.

O, that home of my soul! in my visions and
  dreams,
Its bright jasper wall I can see,
Till I fancy but thinly the veil intervenes,
  Between the fair city and me.

O, how sweet it will be in that beautiful
  land,
  So free from all sorrow or pain,
With songs on our lips, and with harps in
  our hands,
  To meet one another again.

5.

TO the cross of Christ, my Saviour,
  I had brought my weary soul,
Burdened, faint, and broken-hearted,
Praying: "Jesus make me whole."

Cho.—Glory, glory be to Jesus,
  I am counting all but dross,
I have found a full salvation,
  I am resting at the cross.

At the Cross, while prostrate lying,
  Jesus' blood flowed o'er my soul,
All my guilt and sin were covered,
  And he whispered "Child be whole."

At the Cross, I'm calmly trusting,
  Every moment now is sweet:
I am tasting of his glory,
  I am resting at his feet.

6.

I AM coming to the cross,
  I am poor, and weak, and blind;
I am counting all but dross,
  I shall full salvation find.

Cho.—I am trusting, Lord in thee; Blessed
  Lamb of Calvary;
Humbly at thy cross I bow; Jesus
  saves me—saves me now.

Here I give up all to thee,—
  Friends, and time, and earthly store;
Soul and body thine to be—
  Wholly thine—forever more.

In the promises I trust;
  Now I feel the blood applied;
I am prostrate in the dust;
  I with Christ am crucified.

7.

WHO, who are these beside the chilly
  wave,
Just on the borders of the silent grave,
Shouting Jesus' power to save,
  "Washed in the blood of the Lamb?"

Cho.—"Sweeping thro' the gates" of the
  New Jerusalem,
  "Washed in the blood of the Lamb."

These, these are they who, in affliction's
  woes,
Ever have found in Jesus calm repose,
Such as from a pure heart flows,
  "Washed in the blood of the Lamb."

Safe, safe upon the ever shining shore,
Sin, pain, and death, and sorrow, all are o'er;
Happy now and evermore,
  "Washed in the blood of the Lamb."

1.

O, FATHER, let me bear the cross;
Make it my daily food,
Though with it thou dost send the loss
Of every earthly good.

Cho.—I am clinging to the cross,
Yes, I'm clinging, clinging to the cross,
I am clinging to the cross,
Yes, I'm clinging, clinging to the cross.

Take house and lands and earthly fame;
To all I am resign'd;
But let me make one earnest claim;
Leave, leave the cross behind.

I know it costs me many tears;
But they are tears of bliss,
And moments there outweigh the years
Of selfish happiness.

2.

ONE more day's work for Jesus;
One less of life for me!
But heav'n is nearer
And Christ is dearer
Than yesterday to me;
His love and light
Fill all my soul to-night.

Ref.—One more day's work for Jesus,
One more day's work for Jesus,
One more day's work for Jesus,
One less of life for me.

One more day's work for Jesus;
Yes, and a weary day;
But heav'n shines clearer
And rest comes nearer
At each step of the way;
And Christ is all,—
Before his face I fall.

3.

SIMPLY trusting every day,
Trusting thro' a stormy way;
Even when my faith is small,
Trusting Jesus, that is all.

Cho.—Trusting him while life shall last,
Trusting him till earth is past,
Till within the jasper wall—
Trusting Jesus, that is all.

Brightly doth his Spirit shine
Into this poor heart of mine;
While he leads, I cannot fall,
Trusting Jesus, that is all.

Trusting as the moments fly,
Trusting as the days go by,
Trusting him, whate'er befall—
Trusting Jesus, that is all.

4.

ON thee my heart is resting;
Ah! this is rest indeed!
What else, Almighty Saviour,
Can a poor sinner need?
Thy light is all my wisdom,
Thy love is all my stay;
Our Father's home in glory,
Draws nearer every day.

Great is my guilt, but greater
The mercy thou dost give;
Thyself, a spotless offering,
Hast died that I should live.
With thee my soul unfettered
Has risen from the dust;
Thy blood is all my treasure;
Thy word is all my trust.

Through me, thou gentle master,
Thy purposes fulfill;
I yield myself forever
To thy most holy will.
'Tis thou hast made me happy;
'Tis thou hast set me free;
To whom shall I give glory
For ever but to thee!

5.

COME to Jesus, come to Jesus,
Come to Jesus just now,
Just now come to Jesus,
Come to Jesus just now.

He will save you, etc.

He is able, etc.

He is willing, etc.

He is waiting, etc.

He will hear you, etc.

He will cleanse you, etc.

He'll renew you, etc.

He'll forgive you, etc.

If you trust him, etc.

He will save you, etc.

6.

HOW sweet the name of Jesus sounds
In a believer's ear!
It soothes his sorrows, heals his wounds,
And drives away his fear.

Cho.—Help me, dear Saviour, thee to own,
And ever faithful be;
And when thou sittest on thy throne,
Dear Lord, remember me.

It makes the wounded spirit whole,
And calms the troubled breast;
'Tis manna to the hungry soul,
And for the weary, rest.

By thee my prayers acceptance gain,
Although with sin defiled;
Satan accuses me in vain,
And I am owned a child.

7.

COME, every soul by sin oppressed,
There's mercy with the Lord,
And he will surely give you rest,
By trusting in his word.

Cho.—Only trust him, only trust him,
Only trust him now;
He will save you, he will save you,
He will save you now.

For Jesus shed his precious blood
Rich blessings to bestow;
Plunge now into the crimson tide
That washes white as snow.

Yes Jesus is the Truth, the Way,
That leads you into rest;
Believe in him without delay,
And you are fully blest.

9.

TO God—the Father, Son,
And Spirit—Three in One.
All praise be given!
Crown him in every song;
To him your hearts belong;
Let all his praise prolong—
On earth, in heaven.

1.

THERE are songs of joy that I loved to
   sing,
When my heart was as blithe as a bird in
   spring;
But the song I have learn'd is so full of
   cheer,
That the dawn shines out in the darkness
   drear.

Cho.—O, the new, new song, O, the new,
    new song,
   I can sing it now with the ransom'd
    throng,
   Power and dominion to him that shall
    reign;
   Glory and praise to the Lamb that
    was slain.

There are strains of home that are as dear
   as life,
And I list to them oft 'mid the din of strife;
But I know of a home that is wondrous fair,
And I sing the psalm they are singing there.

I shall catch the gleam of its jasper wall,
When I come to the gloom of the even-fall,
For I know that the shadows, dreary and
   dim,
Have a path of light that will lead to him.
         From "Gems of Praise."

2.

MY soul, be on thy guard,
   Ten thousand foes arise;
The hosts of sin are pressing hard,
   To draw thee from the skies.

Cho.—We're marching to Zion,
    The beautiful city of God.

Oh, watch, and fight, and pray,
   The battle ne'er give o'er;
Renew it boldly every day,
   And help divine implore.

Ne'er think the vict'ry won,
   Nor once at ease sit down;
Thy arduous work will not be done,
   Till thou hast got thy crown.

Fight on, my soul, till death
   Shall bring thee to thy God;
He'll take thee at thy parting breath,
   Up to his blest abode.

3.

I SAT alone with life's memories
   In sight of the crystal sea;
And I saw the thrones of the star-crowned
   ones,
With never a crown for me.
And there the voice of the Judge said,
   "Come,"
Of the Judge on the great white throne;
And I saw the star-crowned take their seats,
   But none could I call my own.

I thought me then of my childhood days
   The prayer at my mother's knee—
Of the counsels grave that my father gave,
   The wrath I was warned to flee;
I said, "Is it then too late, too late?
   Shut without must I stand for aye?"
And the Judge, will he say, "I know you
   not."
   Howe'er I may knock and pray?

I thought, I thought of the days of God,
   I'd wasted in folly and sin
Of the times I'd mocked when the Saviour
   knock'd,
   And I would not let him in.
I thought, I thought of the vows I'd made
   When I lay at death's dark door—
"Would he spare my life, I'd give up the
   strife,
   And serve him forevermore.

I seemed as though I woke from a dream
   How sweet was the light of day!
Melodious sounded the Sabbath bells
   From towers that were far away.
I then became as a little child,
   And I wept, and wept afresh;
For the Lord had taken my heart of stone
   And given a heart of flesh.

Still oft I sit with life's memories,
   And think of the crystal sea;
And I see the thrones of the star-crowned
   ones;
   I know there's a crown for me.
And when the voice of the Judge says
   "Come,"
Of the Judge on the great white throne—
I know 'mid the thrones of the star-crowned
   ones,
   There's one I shall call my own.

4.

'MID the deep and billowy ocean,
   Raging now in wild commotion,
All secure, I'm ever singing,
For to Christ my soul is clinging,
Safe amid the tempest's shock,
Resting on the solid rock.

Cho.—On the Rock, on the Rock,
    Resting safely on the Rock:
    On the Rock, the solid Rock,
    Resting safely on the Rock.

What though winds are howling 'round me?
What though darkness now surround me
Threatening utter desolation?
Christ the Rock is my salvation!
Calm amid the wildest shock,
On the everlasting Rock.

With my Saviour, what can harm me?
All hell's legions can't alarm me.
Jesus' mighty arms enclosing,
Sweetly is my soul reposing,
Safe amid the fiercest shock,
On the ever-blessed Rock.

5.

THERE is a gate that stands ajar,
   And through its portals gleaming,
A radiance from the cross afar,
   The Saviour's love revealing.

Ref.—Oh, depth of mercy! can it be
    That gate was left ajar for me?
    For me, for me?
    Was left ajar for me?

That gate ajar stands free for all
   Who seek through it salvation;
The rich and poor, the great and small,
   Of every tribe and nation.

Press onward then, though foes may frown,
   While mercy's gate is open;
Accept the cross, and win the crown,
   Love's everlasting token.

Beyond the river's brink we'll lay
   The cross that here is given.
And bear the crown of life away,
   And love him more in heaven.

110

1.

THE world is overcome
By the blood of the Lamb.

My sins are washed away
In the blood of the Lamb.

I've washed my garments white
In the blood of the Lamb.

I soon shall gain the skies
Through the blood of the Lamb.

2.

HEAVENLY Father, bless me now;
At the cross of Christ I bow;
Take my guilt and grief away,
Hear and heal me now, I pray.

Ref.—Bless me now, bless me now,
Heavenly Father, bless me now!

Now, O Lord! this very hour,
Send thy grace and show thy power;
While I rest upon thy word;
Come and bless me now, O Lord!

Now, just now, for Jesus' sake,
Lift the clouds, the fetters break;
While I look, and as I cry,
Touch and cleanse me ere I die.

3.

THE precious blood of Jesus,
It washes white as snow.

My Saviour, I believe it,
For thou hast made me clean.

Shout, shout the victory,
We're on our journey home.

We'll wear a crown of glory
With Jesus in the sky.

4.

I BRING my sins to thee,
The sins I cannot count,
That all may cleansed be
In thy once open'd fount.

Cho.—Jesus paid it all
All to him I owe,
Sin had left a crimson stain,
He washes white as snow.

My heart to thee I bring.
The heart I cannot read,
A faithless wand'ring thing,
An evil heart indeed.

My life I bring to thee,
I would not be my own;
O Lord, let me be thine,
Be ever thine alone.

5.

GUIDE me, O thou great Jehovah,
Pilgrim through this barren land;
I am weak, but thou art mighty,
Hold me with thy powerful hand:
Bread of heaven, Bread of heaven,
Feed me till I want no more.

Open now the crystal fountain,
Whence the healing waters flow;
Let the fiery, cloudy pillar,
Lead me all my journey through:
Strong Deliverer, Strong Deliverer,
Be thou still my strength and shield.

6.

LORD, I approach the mercy-seat,
Where thou dost answer prayer;
There humbly fall before thy feet,
For none can perish there.

Cho.—I can, and I will, and I do believe
That Jesus died for me.

Thy promise is my only plea;
With this I venture nigh:
Thou callest burdened souls to thee,
And such, O Lord, am I.

O, wondrous love!– to bleed and die,
To bear the cross and shame,
That guilty sinners, such as I,
Might plead thy gracious name.

7.

WELCOME, welcome, dear Redeemer,
Welcome to this heart of mine;
Lord, I make a full surrender,
Every power and thought be thine;
Thine entirely,
Through eternal ages thine.

8.

HO! my comrades see the signal
Jesus waves on high!
Satan's battlements are reeling,
Hear our Captain's cry:

Cho.—"Storm the fort! for I am leading,
I have shown you how;"
Shout the answer back to heaven—
We are ready—*now!*

See! the lofty walls are frowning.
Held by Satan's power;
Sin enshrouds the world in darkness,
Now's the storming hour.

See! the prophets now are showing
How the fort must fall!
There is no such thing as failing,
Shout, my comrades, all!

Fierce and long the siege has lasted,
But the end is near!
Onward leads our great Commander,
Cheer! my comrades, cheer!

9.

'TIS religion that can give
Sweetest pleasures while we live;
'Tis religion must supply
Solid comfort when we die.

After death its joys will be
Lasting as eternity
Be the living God my friend,
Then my bliss shall never end.

10.

PRAISE God from whom all blessings flow,
Praise him, all creatures here below,
Praise him above, ye heavenly host,
Praise Father, Son and Holy Ghost.

INDEX.

ABUNDANTLY able to save,.................... 4
A charge to keep I have................ ... 91
Alas! and did my Saviour bleed?........... 87
Albion C. M. D.,.......... 94
All glory to the bleeding Lamb,... 102
All hail the power of Jesus' name,.... .. 87
Am I a soldier of the cross,................... 87
And can I yet delay?.......................... 91
Are you washed in the blood?... 15
Arise, my soul, arise,..... 95
Arlington C. M.,.............................. 86
At evening time it shall be light,......... 74
Avon, C. M.,................................... 86
Awake, my soul, in joyful lays,........... 85

BADEA, S. M.,................................. 90
Bartimeus, 8, 7,.............................. 98
Behold a stranger at the door,............104
Behold the throne of grace,................ 91
Blessd Jesus, thou art mine,............... 97
By thy birth and by thy tears,..............106

CHEMUNG, L. M.,............................ 82
Children of the heavenly king,........... 93
Christmas, C. M.,............................. 88
Christ's Cross,................................ 78
Come, every soul by sin oppressed,.........108
Come, Holy Ghost, in love,.................. 97
Come, Holy Spirit, calm my mind,......... 85
Come, Holy Spirit, heavenly dove,......... 89
Come, my fond fluttering heart,........... 95
Come, my Redeemer, come,..................103
Come, my soul, thy suit prepare,........... 93
Come, Saviour, Jesus, from above,......... 83
Come, thou fount of every blessing,....... 99
Come to Jesus,................................ 63
Come to Jesus just now,....................108
Come to the Cross,............................ 33
Come, ye sinners, poor and needy,.......... 99
Come, ye that love the Lord,............... 91
Coming to Jesus,.............................. 32
Coronation C. M.,............................ 86
Cressey, C. M.,................................ 86

DEAR Father, to thy mercy-seat,......... 87
Dear Jesus, I long to be perfectly whole, 106
Death and eternity,.......................... 80
Decide to-night,.............................. 47
Deliverance will come,....................... 64
Depth of mercy! can there be?............. 93
Devotion L. M................................. 84
Did Christ o'er sinners weep?.............. 91
Down at the Cross............................. 70
Doxology, C. M............................... 89
Doxology 8, 7, 4,............................110
Doxology, L. M..............................110
Doxology, 7 6 l,.............................100
Doxology 8, 7,................................ 95
Doxology, 6 4,................................106
Doxology, 7, 6,...............................104
Draw me closer to thee,...................... 49
Duke St. L. M................................. 82
Dundee C. M.,................................. 86
Durell 7,...................................... 92

EMMONS C. M.,................................ 88
Enough for me,................................ 72
Evangel 6, 4,................................. 96
Evergreen Plain............................... 14

FAIRMOUNT S. M.,............................ 90
Father, I stretch my hands to thee,   . 89
Forest L. M.,.................................. 84
Forever here my rest shall be,.............. 87
For what are you waiting?.................... 18
From every stormy wind that blows,...... 85

GEBHARDT, 7,..... 92
God is coming,................................ 25
Good news comes o'er the sea,.............. 36
Guide me, O thou great Jehovah,..........110

HALLELUJAH! he redeemed me,......... 29
Hamline, 8, 7,................................ 94
Haste, O sinner, to be wise,................. 93
Hast thou heard of Jesus?................... 45
Have you not a word for Jesus?............. 42
Heavenly Father, bless me now,............110
He leadeth me,................................102
He saves to the uttermost,................... 31
Hiding in the rock,........................... 13
His keeping power,........................... 39
Ho! my comrades, see the signal,..... 110
Horton, 7,..................................... 92
How sweet the name of Jesus sounds,......108
How tedious and tasteless the hours,......106
Hursley, L. M.,............................... 84

I AM coming to the Cross, ...107
I am listening,................................ 56
I am thine own, O Christ,..................104
I bring my sins to thee,.....................110
If thou leadest me,........................... 26
I gave my life for thee,...................... ..103
I have a Saviour, he's pleading in glory,..100
I have entered the valley of blessing,......100
I know not if the dark or bright.............100
I lay my sins on Jesus,.......................101
I left it all with Jesus,......................101
I love to tell the story,......................101
I love the name of Jesus,..................... 72
I'm but a stranger here,......................105
In some way or other the Lord will provide,. 101
Into thy hands, O Lord,...................... 78
In the Christian's home in glory,............102
In the Cross of Christ I glory,............... 89
I shall be satisfied,.......................... 67
I shall be whiter than snow,................. 70
Is my name written there?.................... 27
I sat alone with life's memories.............109
I stand all bewildered with wonder,........104
I thirst, thou wounded Lamb of God,...... 85
I will sing you a song of that beautiful land,..107
I will trust my Redeemer,.................... 7
I would not live without thee,............... 44

JESUS, and shall it ever be?............... 85
Jesus, a word, a look from thee,........... 85
Jesus, I my cross have taken................107
Jesus is passing this way.................... 52
Jesus, lead the way,......................... 77
Jesus, let thy pitying eye,...................106
Jesus, love me still,.......................... 48
Jesus, lover of my soul,...................... 93
Jesus saves me every day,...................105
Jesus, thine all-victorious love,............ 89
Just as I am, without one plea,.............. 83

KNOCKING at the door,...................... 34

LEAD me to Jesus,........................... 10
Lenox, H. M.,................................. 94
Lisbon, S. M.,................................. 90
Lord, dismiss us with thy blessing,......... 99
Lord, I am thine, entirely thine,............ 88
Lord, I approach the mercy-seat,...........110
Lord, I hear of showers of blessing,........105
Lord, we come before thee now,............ 93
Love divine, all love excelling,............. 95
Luton L. M.,.................................. 82

MARTYN, 7 D., ... 92
M Maytown, 8, 7, 4, ... 98
Menr. C. M., ... 88
Melody, C. M., ... 88
My anchor is holding, ... 55
My body, soul and spirit, ... 106
My faith looks up to thee, ... 97
My Father's house, ... 61
My heavenly home is bright and fair, ...105
My hope is built on nothing less, ... 104
My precious Bible, ... 30
My Redeemer lives, ... 37
My soul be on thy guard, ... 109
My spirit is free, ... 43
'Mid the deep and billowy ocean, ... 109

NEARER, my God, to thee, ... 97
N Nearer to me, ... 80
Nearer the Cross, ... 59
'Neath Elim's cooling palms, ... 57
Nettleton, 8, 7, 4, ... 98
No, not despairingly, ... 66
Nothing but the blood of Jesus, ... 78
No time for Jesus, ... 65
Now the solemn shadows darken, ... 99

O, Beulah land, ... 85
O O, bliss of the purified, ... 100
O, come and dwell in me, ... 91
O Father, let me bear the cross, ... 108
O God, forgive the years and years, ... 85
Oh, for a closer walk with God, ... 89
Oh, for a faith that will not shrink, ... 89
Oh, for a heart to praise my God, ... 89
Oh, for a thousand tongues to sing, ... 89
Oh, leave me not alone, ... 60
Oh, that I could repent, ... 91
O Jesus, delight of my soul!, ... 104
O Lord, thy sovereign aid impart, ... 85
One more day's work for Jesus, ... 108
Only waiting, ... 38
O, now I see the crimson wave, ... 107
On thee my heart is resting, ... 108
O, Paradise!, ... 95
Oric. L. M., ... 84
O, take me as I am, ... 74
O, take my fevered hands in thine, ... 83
O, that my loud of sin were gone, ... 83
O, thou God of my salvation, ... 99
O, thou to whose all-searching sight, ... 85
O, to be nothing, ... 104
Our sins on Christ were laid, ... 91

PEACE, 6, 4, ... 96
P Persuaded, ... 76
Pleyel's Hymn, 7, ... 32
Pray without ceasing, ... 54
Precious name, ... 8
Precious promise God hath given, ... 101
Precious Saviour, thou dost save me, ...105

RETURN and come to God, ... 91
R Return, O wanderer, return, ... 87
Rock of Ages, 7, 6 l, ... 96
Rock of Ages, cleft for me, ... 97
Room for Jesus, ... 81
Rosefield, 7, 6 l, ... 96

SAFE in Jesus, ... 51
S Satisfied, ... 66
Saviour, like a shepherd lead us, ... 100
Say sinner, hath a voice within?, ... 85
Seeking for me, ... 41
Send me thy blessing, ... 35
Seymour, 7, ... 82
Shirland, S. M., ... 90
Show pity, Lord, O Lord forgive, ... 83
Sicilian Hymn, 8, 7, ... 98
Sienza, 6, 5, ... 96
Simply trusting every day, ... 108
Sowing the seed by the daylight fair, ... 102

Stand up, stand up for Jesus, ... 90
St. Bernard, C. M., ... 88
Stocking, S, M., ... 90
St. Thomas, S. M., ... 90
Sweet hour of prayer, ... 104
Sweet rivers of redeeming love, ... 95
Sweet the moments, rich in blessing, ... 95

TAKE my life, and let it be, ... 97
T Talking with Jesus, ... 24
Tenderly lead me, ... 68
Tenney, C. H. M., ... 94
Tell me the old, old story, ... 102
That open door, ... 22
The better day coming on, ... 81
The Cross and Crown, ... 19
The Lord is my light, ... 6
The mistakes of my life have been many, 107
The precious blood of Jesus, ... 110
The precious Lamb, ... 17
The prodigal coming home, ... 20
There are songs of joy, ... 109
There is a fountain filled with blood, ... 106
There is a gate, ... 103
There is a land of pure delight, ... 89
There is a spot to me more dear, ... 105
There is joy in heaven, ... 46
There is life for a look, ... 103
There's a highway for the ransomed, ... 103
There's a wideness in God's mercy, ... 100
There's light over there, ... 82
There were ninety and nine, ... 102
'Tis religion that can give, ... 110
The Saviour's call, ... 12
The shadow of the Cross, ... 3
The shining city, ... 55
The sinner's friend, ... 75
The Sun of righteousness, ... 42
The wanderer's prayer, ... 16
The way, the truth, the life, ... 33
The world is overcome, ... 110
This fountain cleanses from all sin, ... 79
This I did for thee, ... 76
This is why I love my Jesus, ... 9
Thou shepherd of Israel and mine, ... 95
To-day the Saviour calls, ... 103
Toiling up the way, ... 5
To the Cross of Christ my Saviour, ... 107
Touch and cleanse me, ... 21
Trusting in the promise, ... 40

VAIN man, thy fond pursuits forbear .. 87

WAITING at the Cross, ... 21
W Warwick, C. M., ... 86
We are singing, ... 60
We are waiting, blessed Lord, ... 95
Webb, 7, 6, ... 98
We praise thee, O God, ... 103
We speak of the realms of the blest .. 101
What a friend we have in Jesus!, ... 103
What means this eager anxious throng?.105
When all thy mercies, O my God, ... 87
When I can read my title clear, ... 87
When I survey the wondrous cross, ... 83
When shall we meet again?, ... 97
When this song of praise shall cease, .. 93
When we all get home, ... 38
Who, who are these beside the chilly wave?. 107
Why don't you come to Jesus?, ... 11
Why don't you receive him?, ... 71
Willie, 8, ... 94
Windham, L. M., ... 82
With tearful eyes I look around, ... 83
Wonderful grace, ... 61
Work before reward, ... 28

YET there is room, ... 105
Y Yield not to temptation, ... 105

www.ingramcontent.com/pod-product-compliance
Lightning Source LLC
Chambersburg PA
CBHW030539270326
41927CB00008B/1444